RUNNING FOR MY LIFE

RUNNING FOR MY LIFE

RUNNING FOR MY LIFE
'From domestic violence to running blind'

Janice Whittle

RUNNING FOR MY LIFE

ISBN: 978-0-6455527-0-6

First published November 2022
©Janice Whittle

All rights reserved. No part of this publication may be reproduced, stored in a retrieval system or transmitted in any form or by any means, electronic, mechanical, photocopying, recording or otherwise, without prior written permission of the publishers.

Published by Janice Whittle

Front & Back Covers – Designed by Janice Whittle

DEDICATION

For every 'Janice'
whose childhood innocence was robbed

RUNNING FOR MY LIFE

Foreword

Born into a life of challenges that includes epilepsy, failed brain surgery robbing her of her vision, her speech, and the use of her right arm and leg coupled with an abusive marriage, Janice is one of those rare people you will never forget.

I have trained soldiers all my life and I have developed a pretty good instinct to read whether or not a person really wants what they are fighting for and whether or not they have the fighting spirit and self-discipline to get there. In that regard, and after getting to know her, I can honestly say Janice is up there with the best of them.

I met Janice when she was 47 years old, and I was an Army officer posted to Weipa. I knew straight away she was something special. My first impression was one of a strong, aggressive woman who didn't take crap from anyone.

The more I talked to her the more I got the impression that Janice knew what she wanted in life but was still working out how to get there. I found out over time that there had been many diversions along the way, but she always returned to [her] main highway of life.

Janice is so good at managing her disabilities that I did not even know for about three months after meeting her that she was legally blind. And she had to tell me. How stupid did I feel.

Whilst most would agree that Janice has every right to centre on her own personal fight at the exclusion of all others, this lady is intent on not only maintaining a good personal social life, but also helping others to break the stigma of isolation.

Many people over the years, including myself, have told Janice she should write this book about her remarkable life, but she has always been scared that such a venture would touch on too many past experiences that would ultimately force her back into a shell, aspects which she needed to leave in the past for her own sanity. I have personally witnessed her crawl into a foetal position whilst reliving events and trying to put them in words. On several occasions, I was wondering if writing this book was such a good idea for her mental health.

Regardless, Janice is ready to share her incredible story and I am proud to write this foreword for the most remarkable person I have ever known. The only other people who even come close to receiving this level of admiration from me are friends, a husband and wife, who were imprisoned in a filthy Laos jail for 12 months and were ultimately released through the efforts of the Australian Government, having never actually been found guilty of anything.

Living up to her motto, "If I can do it, anyone can," this book will take you on a journey that will bring you to laughter and tears, but most of all to a realisation of how strong the human spirit truly is.

MAJOR Bob Varcoe,
MTrgDev, AdvDipThai, DipAWT, DipFM, DipRM, DipGov

RUNNING FOR MY LIFE

PRAISE FOR THE BOOK

The type of characters that we are is coloured and shaped by our history. Some have a history that is difficult or trying and so they colour themselves in hues of blue, black and grey. Others have a history full of joy and validation, and colour themselves from the palette of the rainbow. Yet others, refuse to give into a dark cheerless past and colour themselves from the rainbow adding so much more.

To say that Janice is a colourful character is an understatement, her indefatigable character is undersold by that term. She most certainly is vibrant but this is not borne of a rich past of joy and privilege.

Her story is dark and cheerless, a past which she has not just risen over, rather she has leapt out of the depths and said, "watch out world, here I come!"

I have heard her story as only a psychologist does and seen how she will not give in. The abuse she has been subjected to horrifies me, but of greater impact is the way that she has taken the clichéd pig's ear and woven a silk purse.

I would hope we could all have that strength of character. I recommend that everyone should read a book about such a character; it will most certainly be inspirational. Good luck, Janice in Running for Your Life; I know you'll be the winner.

Raymond Inkpen
Principal Clinical Psychologist

Discovery

Stretching out on my bed, clasping my will in my left hand and my next of kin details in my right, I was sure my final moments on this earth had arrived.

Not wanting to be a burden to the motel staff, I tidied the room before lying down. That way, when they knocked on the door because I had not checked out as planned, it would be easy for them to contact my next of kin. There was nothing I could do about the fright they might have at finding my dead body lying there, but at least the room would be tidy.

My wishes were precise in my will, and the contact numbers were clearly listed. I was calm in my acceptance. I was going to die. Alone. In a motel in Wales. Far from Australia, where I had been taken as a child, and although it was not Ireland, at least it was the land of the Celts, my ancestors.

Illness was nothing new to me, and the last few days I had been here in Wales were more of a struggle than usual.

Although I have no interest in Dr Who, I visited the expo dedicated to the time travelling icon created by British television.

I suppose in ways I am a bit like the Doctor; I have been reborn, I travelled all over and made friends with all sorts of different people, and people have underestimated me, but I have always found my own way to rise up against a challenge.

When I next opened my eyes, 28 hours had passed. It was 6 pm the following evening. Heading for the shower before looking to find a meal to fill my now ravenous rumbling belly, it dawned on me that the reason I had slept so deeply was receiving the news that my divorce had finally been settled.

Across the other side of the world, the court had signed off on the final documentation to make me a free woman, no longer bound by any legal agreement to the man who had been my abuser and tormentor. The relief and stress release had manifested as a much-needed long sleep. I may have slept like the dead, but I was not dying after all.

I had always known I was different. Different to my family and different to the other children at school. I was 7 or 8 when I heard the word epilepsy for the first time.

Mrs Thompson, my third-year teacher, helped me understand why I was different to the other students in my class. I did not know there was anything wrong with me.

Sitting at her orderly and immaculately tidy desk, Mrs Thompson called me to approach. As I stood in front of her, she held out a small stack of booklets. "Take these. And read them when you're at home." I had no idea what she was talking about but because I always did as I was told, I obediently shoved them into my school bag. When I got home, I took out the books that my favourite teacher had given me and curiously examined each of them. I remember there was a small brown one with the word 'Epilepsy' on the cover. There was also a purple pamphlet, 'What Causes Epilepsy?'

Diagnosed at 20 months and averaging seven or eight seizures a day despite the medication, I had no inkling that I was an epileptic.

Everything was hidden from me. Everything. I was kept in the dark. The first simple sentence in that little brown book read, "Epilepsy is a nervous disorder characterised within the brain." This was a moment of revelation, and I was getting a glimpse of the truth about myself, the first discovery of many more to come.

Intently focusing on every word with puzzlement, each detail, from the texture of the cover to the feel of the paper in my little hands, is seared into my memory. How I can remember that when I cannot recall something that happened two seconds ago remains a puzzle to me.

Having devoured the booklet from cover to cover, I went in search of my mother. "Why did Mrs Thompson give me these books?" I held out the booklets to her,

"Oh, don't worry about it." Avoiding looking me in the eye, she dismissively waved her hand to shoo me away.

"Just throw them in the bin." My mother was never overly supportive, but I was perplexed by her dismissal of something my teacher had given me to take home. To my mind, it was like homework. I needed to do as I was told. I had read the booklet but was totally at a loss to understand what the contents had to do with me, and neither could I fathom why my mother would not talk to me about the books.

Despite the instructions my mother had given me, I did not throw the books in the bin. I was usually a good girl doing exactly what I was told as I needed to please everyone and stay out of trouble. This was one of the rare occasions that I disobeyed her. Something inside me would not allow me to carelessly toss aside the information burnt onto those pages as though of no consequence. I could not bring myself to obey; it was as though I knew this was a defining moment.

Years later, I came to understand that I was the secret my parents did not want anyone to know about. They found my condition embarrassing and a secret that needed to be hidden.

With nobody else to ask about my condition, I turned to Mrs Thompson. Talking to her was easy, I felt comfortable with her and asked all the questions that I would have liked my mother to have answered. Through the information my teacher shared, I learnt more about my medical history. I discovered that the little pills I took were to help keep my seizures under control.

My desk at school was positioned at the front of the class and off to the side. It allowed Mrs Thompson to keep me directly in her line of vision; she could keep a close watch on me, and now, with the benefit of hindsight, I understand the reason for the location of my desk was because the school knew I was an epileptic.

I had a lot of trouble trying to comprehend why I was different from my family and why my parents shut down any time I tried to ask any questions.

"Do you want to know a secret?" Mrs Thompson leaned over my desk, peering at me conspiratorially from behind the glasses she always wore. Bobbing my head up and down, I nodded eagerly at my newfound hero as she lowered her voice and whispered conspiratorially, "My name is Janice too." My eyes widened in amazement to hear we shared the same first name.

During my early school years, I had no notion that I was being treated differently because I was epileptic. It is only now, as I look back that I realise what an exceptional teacher Mrs Thompson was. She was the stuff exceptional teachers are meant to be made of. Encouraging, supportive, and there to make a difference in the life of their students, I was never made to feel a burden or embarrassed.

On one occasion, after breaking my arm during an epileptic fit, I returned to school with my right arm in a sling. It was almost impossible for me to write, which made me anxious and frustrated; Mrs Thompson gently encouraged me to try using my left hand.

Feeling valued, listened to, and supported, I thrived during my time in class with Mrs Thompson. My curiosity and love of learning were fanned into life through my experience in her class. The fact that I can remember her name over 40 years later is a testament to her skill as a teacher who was clearly dedicated to helping her pupils learn.

Family

Growing up, I learnt that being part of a family meant being abused both verbally, physically, and sexually. At the time, I did not know there was a term for what was happening to me. As children, whatever we are exposed to and surrounded by in our own families becomes normal. We accept what is happening to us because we know nothing outside of our surroundings. It was not until many years later that I came to the realisation that my childhood experiences were far from normal.

My parents worked for pharmaceutical companies, my mother in the warehouse picking and packing, and my father as a truck driver doing the deliveries. In the school holidays, it was my father that looked after me. He would put me in his big white truck and take me on his rounds. They were all local deliveries which meant we were home every evening.

I was about 5 or 6 when the abuse started in the confines of the truck cab. The vinyl seats rubbed against my naked bottom as he fondled and probed me. I became immune to the pain, and the relaxant drugs for my epilepsy ensured my docile acceptance of what was happening.

This pattern continued for many years. As I got older, I stayed in school for longer hours in an attempt to avoid going home. It became my habit to sleep with my bedroom door open and the corridor light on; an open door made me feel safer. It made it more difficult for my father to creep into my room, as my bedroom door being closed was highly unusual.

Both my maternal grandfather and father modelled abusive behaviour while the women in my family held their tongues. It did not matter what was happening in front of them, no one said a word, and I learnt from an early age to keep my eyes down and my mouth shut.

I avoided my grandfather, a hulkingly, solid beast of a man whose massive hands routinely came down with brute force on the body of my petite, kind and gentle-natured grandmother. I do not remember when my grandparents moved in or even why, but I know they came from England to live in a caravan in our backyard. The regular sounds of the beatings dished out to my grandmother and her soft sobs permeated through the thin fibro walls that separated the caravan, which was parked smack bang tight up against the side of our house. There was little room for privacy with paper-thin walls.

Once he had finished belting her, I would hear the key turning in the lock of the caravan before seeing his heavy frame amble in the direction of the pub. No one ever dared say a word or lift a finger to stop him. Nor did I have the courage to knock on the locked door to check if Grandma was okay.

The lesson I learnt was that the men in the family had every right to do as they pleased with the women in the family.

My mother stood meekly by. Her silence condoned the behaviour. We never discussed what was happening to either my grandmother or myself. I did not know it at the time, but now, as an adult, when I think back to my childhood, I am convinced that my grandmother knew that my father was sexually abusing me.

On one occasion, my grandmother suggested taking me to

England to meet family and then on to Ireland to meet my Irish relatives. My mother's vehement "No!" ended the discussion before it had even had a chance to get started. I believe this was my grandmother's way of trying to remove both herself and me from the destructive and abusive men in our lives.

    Children have few opportunities in their early formative years to learn from people outside of their families; it was natural to believe that the life I was living was normal. I learnt that I had no say or control over my own body and lost the ability to feel connected; it was too frightening to face what was happening. Combining my family circumstances with the prescription drugs for my epilepsy meant that I existed in a foggy haze with little ability to feel connected or present. From my parents and grandfather, I learnt that hurting and inflicting pain on each other was the normal way for a family to act.

    It has taken most of my adult life to unlearn the relationship lessons from my upbringing. The trauma that was inflicted turned me into someone who is extremely wary of relationships. It felt unnatural to have emotions, and I did not trust them. Going step by step, slowly and carefully, I gradually eased into a place where I now trust my instincts and know that healthy love is built on mutual respect, honesty and, above all, trust. It is not built on fear.

I was about 9 when, through my grandmother's question about taking me to meet family in Ireland, I finally discovered I was adopted. Finding out was, in a way, a relief, as I knew I was not like my parents or brother. On a physical level, I looked totally different, and from an emotional perspective, there was no connection, but at the time, I did not give this much thought. In my heavily medicated state, I was not really capable of thinking clearly, although there were occasional flashes when I had moments of clarity.

I never knew my birth mother, but I did discover that I was born in Ireland. I am a statistic; one of the 57,000 babies from the shameful era in Catholic Irish history that lasted from 1920 through to 1998, when unmarried mothers in Ireland were forsaken by society and sent away to be hidden from the world until the baby arrived. The unwed mother then returned to her life without the baby, and her great shame was never spoken of again. I was born at the largest of Ireland's nine mother and baby homes, St Patrick's Mother & Babies Home, in Dublin on St Patrick's Day. I came to Australia at two years old with my adoptive English parents.

By the time I got to high school, the medication dosage had increased. I was a zombie, totally zoned out on medication as my father continued his sexual abuse whenever the opportunity arose.

My medication dosage, dispensed in sets of 2's – an anti-convulsant and a muscle relaxant – came in a little red pill case. Each day at 7 am, 2 pm and again at 9 pm, I obediently took my pills which made me totally pliable and docile. Years later, when I finally subpoenaed my medical file to sue for medical negligence, it was there in black and white that I was purposely being given a dosage above the legal limit of the medication.

It was touch and go as to whether I could graduate high school, as the school was reluctant to allow me into the science laboratories.

My seizures, which happened frequently, were unpredictable and made me a liability. Mr Lyons, the science teacher, became my unlikely champion. He reminded me of a mad professor because he always wore odd socks which stuck out as his pants legs rode up when he was sitting at the desk. He knew I needed to complete science to get my school leaving certificate.

My parents did not take any active part in my schooling; it was thanks to Mr Lyons, who spoke to support my case, that I was admitted into the science class. It did mean that he had to watch me like a hawk, especially when it came to using the Bunsen burners. I was only allowed to use them under strict supervision in case I had a seizure.

The Medical Merry Go Round

Although I do not have a completely clear recollection of all that I went through in terms of my childhood treatment, doctors were a constant in my life up until I finally managed to become independent and free from the grasp of prescription drugs. I avoided drawing attention to myself because I was terrified of being noticed.

Shy, timid, and afraid whenever I was questioned or approached, my protection mechanism involved scrunching myself up and shrinking as small as possible. Trying to hide myself my logic was that if no one could see me, if they did not notice me, I would be safe.

My actions are confirmed in the copy of a video that the hospital filmed of me over a period of one week when I was 19 years old. I was confined to a bed for an entire week, hooked up to the EEG machine and television monitor so they could record all my seizures, body movements and actions for an entire week.

The dates were 21 October to 28 October 1989, with the final video filmed at 17.30. I obtained a copy of this video, together with my other medical records, through Freedom of Information when I was planning to sue for medical negligence.

Following the video recording, Dr Sommerville told my parents that I should have the Wada test. The test, named after Juhn Wada from Japan, was originally an experiment in the late 1940s to look at language and schizophrenia. He figured out a way to put half the brain to sleep and talk to the other so that he could find out which side of the brain was affecting various functions and language.

In the 1960s, the test was adapted for use to assess suitability for epilepsy surgeries. Once it dawned on me exactly what was going to be involved with the brain surgery and, more importantly, the risk that was involved, I surprised everyone by refusing the surgery that was being recommended. I am not sure who was more surprised, the medical team or myself.

Because of all the prescription medication, I frequently struggled to properly understand what was happening around me.

In my zombie-like state, I was compliant and simply doing as I was told without considering that there might be other options. Not wanting to draw attention to myself, I would rarely think to ask questions. It was pretty much unheard of that the good girl that I was would actually speak up for what I wanted. Head bowed and eyes to the floor, I meekly accepted whatever was coming my way.

Yet somehow, somewhere deep inside of me was a well of resistance that gushed into life when I heard the words, "If we do brain surgery, there is a high possibility you will lose your sight. You may lose the function of your right arm and leg, and you will lose your speech."

Something about how those words were delivered permeated into the fog of my mind; a glimmer of understanding sparked, and I spoke up. I found my inner voice and decided that I would rather live with my epilepsy than face the chance that I was going to be little more than a vegetable.

At 19 years old, I was legally an adult who could make my own decisions. The fact that I had not asserted my rights, spoken up or fought back on any occasion where I was abused, coerced, or told to do something I knew was wrong made it even more shocking that I would defy the wishes of my parents and my treating medical professional. Compliant Janice, who always did as she was told was speaking up and making her voice heard. I am not sure who was more shocked, them or me. This was the first glimmer of my rebellious nature that had been dormant my entire life.

No matter how they tried to persuade me, I was adamant that I would not consent to have surgery. I was not going to agree to have the operation, and that was the end of the matter. After leaving the hospital, I gave the conversation no further thought. Out of the blue, I received a telephone call at work; the voice at the other end was from the hospital. They were insistent that I had an appointment and was supposed to be at the hospital for admission.

Perplexed, I asked, "What am I being admitted for?"

The receptionist, sounding exasperated, explained that I was booked in for surgery the next day. She stressed that I needed to complete the pre-admission and was holding everything up with my non-arrival. I explained there was a misunderstanding; I was not having any surgery.

Despite trying to remember, I cannot recall the exact details of how it transpired that despite the fact I had refused the surgery, I was collected from work, forcibly dragged out of the office, and escorted to the hospital against my will.

No one would listen to me. No one came to help. I will never ever forget that day. Kicking and screaming at the top of my lungs proved futile as four men in white coats physically restrained me. I knew that they were going to put me under the knife despite the fact I had not given my consent. I was a drugged-up puppet, a vulnerable young woman with no one in my corner. They were going to do as they wished. I was dispensable.

Unceremoniously jabbed with a needle that rendered me unconscious. I have no idea how long I was out for. When I came around, I was immobile, unable to move an inch. At first, I did not understand where I was or what had happened. I did not have a clear picture.

As I became more awake, fear rose in my throat as I attempted to roll over. The resistance I felt was the restraining bands biting into my arms, trying to move my legs, yielding the same resistance; I realised I was strapped to a hospital bed. The firmness of my binding would not yield no matter how much thrashing and flaying about I attempted to break free.

The bonds held fast; I was tied down like an animal in captivity. Tears streamed down my face as I lay terrified, gripped by fear of what was to happen to me. I knew I was going to die. Alone. I eventually must have fallen asleep.

Whether I was given further medications, I have no idea. When I opened my eyes again, it was morning. Tuesday 20th of February 1990, the date is imprinted indelibly in my memory; I forget many things, but that date is one I will never ever forget no matter how long I live. A nurse was standing over me with a trolly. She was waiting to shave my head. My long red hair fell away as they prepared me for brain surgery. In less than 10 minutes my locks were gone, and my head bare.

They were going to operate on me without my consent. I was a guinea pig for a surgery that held no hope for me. In my subpoenaed medical files, it clearly states "even successful surgery will not help".

A team of 6 doctors were gathered in the operating theatre and the last thing I remember was the voice of the neurologist saying, "It's time to put you to the test".

When I awoke, it was to total blackness. I had no vision. I could not talk. I could not move. I simply existed in a state of limbo at the mercy of those who were supposed to be caring for me.

When the groggy effects of the anaesthetic began to wear off, my ears tuned in to the sounds that surrounded me.

Despite my lack of sight, my heightened senses brought forward consciousness of my surroundings; the awareness dawned.

I was in a ward with five elderly men. There were no gentle sounds or soft murmurs of women's voices.

The raucous laughter, the groans and the chatter all came from male voices.

Awaking the next morning after a totally restless sleep, interrupted by the soft hum and beeps of electronic hospital machinery, I looked around me and could make out the privacy curtain hanging from a track on the ceiling.

Relief coursed through my body as I realised that I could see a little. I had not gone blind. My eyes had been swallowed up into the blown-up beach ball that was my post-surgery face.

As the swelling went down, my eyes emerged, and my vision started to return. It was not 100%, I had lost my peripheral vision, but I did have tunnel vision, which was better than no vision. I was grateful to have some sight.

Feeling as though my heart would burst from my chest with the fear pounding through my veins, I realised that neither my arms nor legs could move.

As hard as I tried to lift my arm, it lay motionless. Flat and useless. With increasing levels of panic, I desperately tried to wiggle my toes. Nothing.

Tears coursed down my swollen face as I lay on that hard hospital bed, only to be interrupted by a male nurse who drew aside the privacy curtains, picked me up like a sack of potatoes and carried me through into the shower room.

The hospital gown that affords no privacy was roughly bunched up as he proceeded to rape me on the cold, hard tiles as my screams went unheard.

My head, swaddled in bandages with 87 staples across my skull, reverberated with the noise of my own screams as fear clawed at my throat. No one came to rescue me. I was alone.

Following the craniotomy and left temporal lobectomy, I was unceremoniously discharged from the hospital; kicked out. The medical team did not want to see me again. They were washing their hands of me.

My prognosis was grim. I was told that it would be impossible for me to live past the age of 25. I had five years left to live if I was lucky.

I felt then, and I still feel now, that I had been a total guinea pig, abandoned when things went wrong and left without any follow-up, rehabilitation, counselling, therapy, or anything that may have helped me cope.

The first time I had access to physiotherapy was not until after July 2013, over 20 years after my surgery.

I was living in Newcastle, New South Wales. The Hunter area became a trial site for the National Disability Insurance Scheme (NDIS). I was one of those who went on the trial, and under that plan, I received funding enabling me to receive the support I needed. I consider myself lucky that I was living in an area that happened to be the largest trial site out of those rolled out and that when the trial period ended in July 2016, the full NDIS was rolled out across Australia.

*****

Bringing me home from the hospital, my father carried me inside and unceremoniously dumped me on the bed that had been mine since childhood. Lying there, on top of the pink doona cover, I realised that the word family did not apply to me. No words of comfort came from my mother, no offers of help. I had no family. I was too much trouble.

As I lay there alone, my eyes, swollen from a combination of crying and the operation, fixed on the large blurry, yet familiar shape of my white wardrobe opposite the bed. The shape brought me comfort as it was familiar. It became a landmark that allowed me to recognize where I was whenever I woke from my uneasy sleep.

It was lying there, in the twilight state of semi-consciousness, that I became aware of the harsh reality that I was a burden. I think I always knew that I was not truly wanted, but up until this moment, I had not considered that I was an actual burden. With the use of both my right arm and leg gone, if I were to have any hope at all of recovery, it would be down to me to work out how to get myself mobile.

Rolling to the edge of the bed, I tried to stand up. I fell. Dragging myself up off the floor by using my good arm to leverage against the bed, I fell again.

There was no one to help. My parents were at work, so it was down to me. Eventually, after a supreme effort that took all of the strength I could muster, I managed to traverse across my room and through to the toilet that, as luck would have it, was next to my room.

My daily routine involved slapping my useless leg and arm, applying heat packs and doing anything and everything I could think of in an attempt to bring sensation back into my useless limbs. It worked.

After a few weeks of my own brand of physiotherapy, I was able to awkwardly stumble about like a drunk. I had managed to push my broken body to respond, to move again, despite being told it would be impossible. They had written me off, but I had other ideas.

As the swelling around my face gradually subsided, the realisation that my vision had been affected became obvious; I had perfect tunnel vision. What was directly in front of me was crystal clear, but everything else was gone.

Although the operation was performed because of my epilepsy, the

Epilepsy Association could offer me no support, saying I did not fit their criteria and that my vision problem meant I needed to approach the Royal Blind Society, whose answer was that the vision loss was related to my epilepsy which meant they were unwilling to fund support for me. The bouncing back and forth between associations went on for several years; it all came down to the funding dollars that each was preciously guarding. I was the victim who fell between the cracks. I did not fit neatly into any of the buckets.

    I was so busy focusing on my recovery, regaining mobility and being independent that I never gave a thought to myself as a person. My ability to do basic physical tasks like walking, bathing, and dressing myself were where I was concentrating. As far as I was concerned, I still had perfect vision. What I could see was perfect. I had lost my peripheral vision from surgery and had tunnel vision, but I could see what was in front of me perfectly.

    I willingly admit as I look back now, that I really was not all there mentally, not the full quid. When I think about it, I suspect it was because I refused to accept the prognosis I was given. The logical part of what I was being told did not make sense to me. Instead, I found an inner determination and somehow managed to tap into my own strength, a strength I did not know I possessed, to aid my own mobility recovery.

During this time of recovery, which stretched over many years, Bruce Graf, a psychologist, was doing an Eye Movement Desensitisation and Reprocess Therapy (EMDR), a form of treatment that was relatively new and focused directly on the memory, on me. The intention was to change the way that the memory is stored in the brain and reduce or eliminate the problematic symptoms. The EMDR sessions did not go well because it was just messing with my head. Bruce decided to stop the EMDR sessions and replace them with normal psychology appointments.

After many sessions, he gently explained, "You have two serious issues. Number one is there is a little girl inside of you that's trying to get out. Secondly, your biggest problem is you are grieving your own death."

I had no idea what on earth he was talking about and actually thought to myself, "You're an idiot. I'm alive. I've got a heartbeat. You're definitely an idiot."

Fortunately for me, he persisted. During additional sessions, I gradually became more receptive as he gently led me on an exploration of what he perceived as my two main issues. He explained that the little girl who was abused was trying to release her anger and get over her experience.

When it came to grieving my own death, he explained, "The sweet, innocent Janice who went into the theatre died on the bed in the surgical ward theatre. But this other person took over her body and replaced her. Her name is Janice too, but she's very angry. She's very straightforward."

I was now stuck with the new Janice "You have to learn how to cope with it. To cope with the differences from being very sweet, innocent, shy, you know, a little angel to being someone who must stand on their own two feet, who has to defend herself, who has to learn the basics in life; like walking and talking and to be able to hold a conversation."

It took me several months of sessions to process and fully understand what he said. I was in my mid 20's, but I clearly recall exactly what he looked like. He was nothing special to look at; an average-looking Caucasian male with light brown greying hair and glasses. You would not look at him twice walking down the street.

I have lost track of exactly how many medical professionals I have seen in my lifetime, and yet, even though my sessions with Bruce Graf took place over 30 years ago, I remember him for one simple reason. He turned on a switch that shed illuminating light on the emotional crisis, the sadness and the anger that I had bottled up internally; he actually helped me by making a positive difference in my life. It was through his dedication and persistence that I was able to eventually understand the jumbled, conflicting emotions that I was processing. He was not an idiot, after all.

With the encouragement of my husband, which was more like a case of constantly having a go at me, I decided to seek legal action against the hospital for medical negligence.

Beginning to walk down this path, I found myself in further trouble, which led to me developing an even more serious case of iatrophobia, the irrational fear of doctors, than I already had. To this day, I continue to be plagued by the fear of doctors.

Shortly after speaking to Legal Aid, I was picked up by the police and taken to a psychiatric hospital. One of the doctors involved in my brain surgery operation was the head honcho of the local psychiatric facility where I was forcibly admitted. I was tormented and locked up for imagining I had brain surgery; I believe this was done by medical professionals in an attempt to discredit or frighten me away from my course of action.

I was admitted on a Tuesday, and all patients faced a magistrate on Wednesday. On admission, I was taken to a padded cell where two male nurses sat on me to stop me from trying to squirm free of their hold; one injected something into my buttocks. Locked up alone and frightened, I remained in the padded cell for 24 hours. By the time I was released from my prison and returned to the regular wing of the hospital, it was too late to face a magistrate. Missing the opportunity that Wednesday meant confinement for yet another long week until the magistrate returned.

A Legal Aid solicitor came in to represent each patient. When it was my turn to face the magistrate. I sat frozen in shock as the reasons for holding me in a padded cell were read out. My ears could hardly comprehend the words I was hearing "imagining she had undergone brain surgery, seeing pink elephants in the sky and hearing the trees talk to her."

Years of abuse and hiding my emotions meant I could keep my voice steady despite the almost crippling fear that gripped me. They had the power to lock me up, and I needed to demonstrate that I was sane.

"I know that the operation did happen as I have the scars, the injuries, the memories, and the paperwork." I forced the words past the constriction in my throat, clearly articulating to the magistrate that none of the accusations were true.

The drill hole scars on my head proved unmistakably clear evidence that brain surgery was not a figment of an overly vivid imagination filled with pink elephants and talking trees. Keeping a tight hold on my pent-up rage at the outrageous lies concocted, I managed to convince the magistrate to look further into my case.

OPERATION PERFORMED: Left temporal lobectomy.

PROCEDURE: With the patient supine and the head turned toward the right, a left Falconer flap was turned. The temporalis muscle was turned down with the skin and a free bone flap raised. The dura was opened. There was no superficial middle cerebral vein and no sylvian fissure to be identified. The temporal lobe was retracted superiorly and the inferior middle and a thickened Superior temporal gyrus were identified. A 5cm temporal lobectomy was performed sparing the superior temporal gyrus. There was no Labbe vein identified.

Similarly, on the hemispheric suction, the temporal horn of the lateral ventricle could not be found. An en bloc excision of the temporal lobe down to the incisura was undertaken. There was no obvious tumour. The specimen was sent for pathological examination.

After attention to haemostasis the wound was closed in layers over a suction drain. Autoclips were used for the skin.

Once the irrefutable evidence was presented, the magistrate ordered my immediate release. The magistrate also spoke to the Legal Aid solicitor about a possible case of medical negligence being held against the hospital, health service and the individual doctors involved.

The fear and memories of what I had experienced in the hospital vividly flashed through my incomplete and damaged brain; my terror, combined with the fact that I might lose everything, including my home, held me back. I never proceeded with my negligence case, and the statute for any action has long since passed.

Today, I have the medical reports, the videos, and a mountain of other documentation that explain what happened to me; it is how I can remember and know that none of this is a figment of my imagination. Solid hard evidence is in my own hands.

Whilst writing this memoir, I have referred to my medical history to confirm details that, due to my memory loss, are not so clear, and at times, it is like being a voyeur looking in on the life of someone else.

What happened was a lifetime ago, and yet, for my self-preservation, I have made the deliberate decision to keep the names of the hospitals, doctors, and health services out of this memoir.

My fear of repercussions, together with the kaleidoscope of nightmares that continue to haunt me of the abusive treatment I received at the hands of medical authorities, people who are, by virtue of their chosen profession and formal studies, entrusted with the care of patients and have sworn an oath to do no harm.

In 1948, the World Medical Association, in the Declaration of Geneva, as a direct result of Nazi physicians conducting barbarous medical experiments, added this promise "never to act contrary to the laws of humanity."

My experiences have shown that this was not adhered to when it came to my treatment.

Because of the actions taken by the medical team, my life was forever changed, my mobility was hindered, and I was declared legally blind.

****

The definition of legally blind, as explained by Vision Australia, is "A person is considered legally blind if they cannot see at six metres what someone with normal vision can see at 60 metres or if their field of vision is less than 20 degrees in diameter. Government departments use the term 'legally blind' to define a person whose degree of sight loss entitles them to special benefits."

The Lifting Fog

Being enveloped in brain fog was a natural state of being for me, thanks to all my medications. Following my surgery, where I ended up with an acquired brain injury (ABI), it was hard to predict what was going to happen to me.

The long terms effects vary from person to person. I needed to undergo a formal assessment to see what the possibilities were for my life.

The surgery affected both my cognitive and physical abilities. This is common for many people with an ABI.

The longer-term effects for me have been a slowing down in how fast I am able to process information, and I have lost sensory abilities, including the sense of taste, touch and smell.

I had already been declared legally blind after having an assessment at Royal Blind Society which is now known as Vision Australia.

No one was clear on what they were going to do with me. Would I need to go into a home or was there a chance I could live independently?

At no point did it occur to anyone to ask my opinion or bother to find out what I might want to do. No longer being overdosed on medication, I was envisaging an opportunity to attempt to create a new chapter in my life.

Finally free from the doped up, drugged out haze, thanks to supposedly well-meaning medical professionals, I did have a slightly clearer perspective. The fog, from my perspective, had started to lift. With a little more sense of what I did and did not want to do, I thought that it might be worth trying to study something. I felt I had the potential to make something of myself and wanted to have the opportunity.

Sitting at the little round table in an interview room at the Commonwealth Rehabilitation Service (CRS) offices in Parramatta, the assessor barely glanced at me as she walked into the room clutching a bundle of paperwork. I presumed they were the reports from the assessment tests I had been run through. Taking her seat, she rifled through her papers before putting them to one side.

Folding her arms across her chest and looking at me as though I was a specimen under a microscope, she announced, "You are so dumb you won't even pass a Certificate of Attainment."

Flinching as she bit out those dreadful words, I swallowed the lump that was rising in my throat; anguished pain tore through me at the realisation she was putting me into a box marked "useless" and slamming the lid on tight.

Being told, in no uncertain terms, that I was dumb did absolutely nothing for my already low sense of self-worth. Her brutal, cruel words continue to reverberate in my head to this day. And yet, simultaneously, a switch to an invisible well of determination inside me flicked on. The hard plastic chair made me want to physically wriggle to get more comfortable, yet I sat still as she droned on. I was not going to give her the satisfaction of a reaction. Her words fell on deaf ears. I defiantly made up my mind that I was going to prove the bitch wrong.

Rather than trying to facilitate my ability to live as normal a life as possible despite my disability, I was being pigeonholed and prejudged based on some antiquated system filled with prejudices. I was an epileptic with an ABI, and therefore, in the eyes of the authorities, was written off as next to useless, which was confirmed by the way my assessment was handled and how dismissively I was treated by the assessor.

Filled with steely determination, I began to look at what possibilities were open to me. I discovered that the local college ran a series of evening courses. Short courses on a myriad of topics. The tuition fees were reasonable. I decided to pay them myself rather than tap into funding that was available to me. I wanted to be totally in control and meeting the costs out of my own pocket meant that the agreement and my enrolment were strictly between the college and myself. I did not need to report on my progress or outcomes, and no one had a right to any information on my registration. It was strictly my business. My logic was that if I failed, no one would know.

I'd always had a talent for craft which made me decide to choose picture framing as my first course. I loved every aspect of the 8-week course and looked forward to each lesson. They were only for 2 hours, so concentration was not an issue.

A frisson of pride filled me when I received my first Statement of Attainment; I had completed the course.

In case it was a fluke, I immediately enrolled in a colour, style and imaging course, followed by a beauty course. Studying opened a whole new world to me. I was in my element, eagerly looking forward to each of the lessons.

Holding the Statement of Attainment for each of the courses I had successfully completed in my own two hands allowed my confidence to begin to soar.

The assessor was wrong. I felt like marching down to her office and confronting her. It would have been immensely satisfying to walk in, slap down my Statements of Attainment and say, "You were wrong, bitch! Completely wrong. I am not dumb after all." I resisted the temptation and came to the realisation that the tests they ran were not the right kind of tests for me. I think of this as being similar to how not all children are suited for traditional classroom learning. Clearly, I was not suited for the traditional run-of-the-mill tests they were running on everyone with an acquired brain injury and epilepsy.

Confidence restored and feeling ready to tackle the next level of challenges; I set my sights higher to enrol at Technical and Further Education college (TAFE) in a certificate course; a step up from a statement of attainment. I knew that doing a certificate would mean I needed extra concentration, and I might also need additional support.

Visiting the Disability Co-Ordinator at Blacktown, New South Wales, TAFE, I explained I wanted to enrol in their advertising course and that I had started my own business, a small craft shop, because no one would give me a job.

Next followed an interview with the Head of the Department, who explained that I would be better off studying marketing to begin with as I would get more immediate value for my business. He was also brutally honest about his concerns, "Look, we've never had a student like you before. You have so many different, you know, conditions and issues." I respected him for his honestly.

"It doesn't matter because I've never studied marketing before. So, we're both on the same page." was my cheeky response.

I breathed a huge sigh of relief when the admissions paperwork was completed.

The Department Head was right; what I learnt in the marketing course has served me extremely well in the years that have elapsed.

In fact, it has helped me create and understand the nuances that are needed to market this book. Continuing with my TAFE education, I racked up several additional certificates as well as an International Computer Driver's Licence that I completed in two weeks. It was supposed to be a three-month self-paced course. The shocked teacher said, "You are way above everyone else. You can stay the three months, and I'm just going to let you do some of our other courses." I well and truly got a lot of certificates out of that, proving to myself yet again how wrong the assessor was.

It was finally time to stop enrolling in courses. I had proved my point.

I could do anything I set my mind to. It might not be easy, but almost anything was possible if I was determined enough.

Determination is my middle name, especially when I am told I cannot do something!

From the Frying Pan into the Fire

At 15, I got my first job; it was at an aquarium. I then moved on to a 12-month traineeship with the New South Wales government at the Department of Agriculture - Biological and Chemical Research Institute. It was specifically tailored for people who were not so likely to be employed because of disabilities. I worked three days a week and went to Granville TAFE to study for two days a week.

After 12 months, I moved on to working for the New South Wales Council for Intellectual Disability at Denistone East before getting a job at Industrial Laminators. My job in the office involved going up and down the stairs of the two-story building which housed the office upstairs and the factory downstairs.

I was still living at home with my parents as there was no way I could afford to move out.

When the initial discussions began about the possibility of having surgery for my epilepsy, my boss, Eddie, wanted to let me go immediately.

He was thinking that anyone who had brain surgery would not be able to work properly. In hindsight, he was right, but I argued persuasively that I had sick leave to use; eventually I wore him down and Eddie agreed to allow me to use my sick leave. I managed to keep my job.

The man whom I ended up marrying was the forklift driver at Industrial Laminators. Purely by coincidence, I bumped into him one evening out at the pub, it was not too long after my surgery. Despite being shaved off for the operation, my flaming red hair had grown back, making me easy to spot in a crowd and he clearly remembered me. Over a drink we started getting to know each other as individuals rather than simply someone from work.

"Pack your bags and move in with me." My heart leapt with joy; his words sounded like music to my ears. We had to keep our relationship a secret as it was frowned on at work for the staff to be involved with each other.

Being starved of any kind of affection from my parents, I found his attention to me flattering. The adopted little girl buried deep inside of me was desperate to belong, to have a family that I fit into, instead of being the outsider. I felt I was being offered a lifeline, a way out of the home that I never belonged in. I could not move out fast enough. I thought I was gaining a newfound freedom; I would have a home of my own.

Fighting my way back to recover from the surgery robbed me of the ability to properly function at work. I could not go up and down the stairs between the factory floor and office with ease and was struggling to focus on the tasks I was meant to complete. I came to the conclusion that I needed to resign from Industrial Laminators as I could no longer do my job. I would rather leave under my own steam than be sacked.

It took every ounce of effort I could muster to make my scrambled brain and non-functioning limbs complete basic daily tasks. I battled to get through each day and was highly vulnerable.

The house I moved into, the place where I was expecting to start my new life of freedom, was a shabby cladded two-bedroom one bathroom house with walls that desperately needed painting and stained carpets. It seemed like heaven to me for the simple reason that it was to be my own home. A place where I would be able to be myself.

My husband had paid $55,000 for the house using a payout he received, but once I moved in, he immediately changed the title into both our names. At the time, I felt it was his way of creating more security for me. It was only later that I grasped how calculated his move was.

I was receiving a blind pension, which meant I was eligible for discounts on electricity, rates, gas and much more. You do not have to have a driving licence to be able to own a car, which meant that even though I could not drive, I had a car registered in my name because it meant free registration.

I thought I had met the man of my dreams. It took me a terribly long time to understand that the man I thought was wonderful and the route I had chosen as an escape from the abuse I was experiencing at my childhood home was in fact a jump from the frying pan into the fire.

Finding myself pregnant with my first child filled me with excitement, and at the same time, with dread. I wanted to be able to look after the baby. I made the decision to go cold turkey off my medications the moment I found out I was pregnant. My concern was for the potential side effects associated with my anti-seizure medications. I knew that the risk factors appeared to increase with higher doses.

I had been on medication since I was two years old, I was afraid for the unborn life growing inside me. I worried that my baby was at risk from the drugs that had been pumped through my body for the best part of twenty years; I would rather fit constantly for nine months than endanger my baby. I wanted to be a good mother. I was determined to love this baby; I would be all that my own mother had not been. Despite frequent fitting during the pregnancy, I delivered a healthy baby son.

Coming off the medication was a revelation; the unexpected bonus was that I found I had a personality. Having the drugs out of my system meant I started to develop independent thought, the fog that had started to lift earlier receded completely. I was turning into someone I did not know had existed previously; my independence started to kick in. I began to think for myself and to ask more questions. I had, up to this point, never truly laughed in my life. I had been an empty shell that merely existed. I began to understand that life could actually be fun. I desperately wanted to be able to enjoy living life to the fullest.

As our family was growing, we took out a loan to renovate the house. I had my little business, the craft shop and my blind pension, which was not means tested. We were able to pay off the loan quickly. When the renovations were finished, the house had been converted into a five-bedroom two story home complete with an office, a rumpus room and a second bathroom. It was completely transformed from the original shabby, run down house I had originally moved into.

I had two children before we decided to get married. The decision to legalize our relationship was mutual, with the driving force for me being that I yearned for us to be a real family, and in my mind, that meant us all sharing the same surname. I desperately wanted to belong.

I became Janice Waters. In hindsight, that was one of the worst decisions I have ever made. The moment the marriage certificate was signed, my husband morphed into someone I did not recognise. He became a man with the attitude that his wife was his property.

"You are mine. I own you," were the words he used.

I was 23 years old and 100% controlled by my husband. I was no longer allowed to dress up or wear makeup. The rule he went by was that if you were not born with it, you were not allowed to wear it. His bizarre rule went as far as including deodorant and hair products.

To ensure I was dressed to the rules of what my husband considered appropriate, he would buy my clothes. I was not allowed to go to the shops and choose what I wanted. Wearing what I was given, my wardrobe consisted of track pants and the matching Sloppy Joe top. The drab beige colour ensured that I always looked washed out, which, combined with the fact that each of the outfits was always at least a size too large, I ended up looking larger than I was; a frumpy and unattractive woman whom no one would give a second glance, except perhaps one of pity.

I also no longer had my own bank account. Stupidly, in my desire to belong and be a real family, I had agreed to close my account. As a married couple, we shared a joint account; my name might have been on the account, but he fully controlled it. I had no means of accessing any money. I was naïve and innocent; it never crossed my mind to speak up and insist on keeping my own bank account for my blind pension to go into.

Entirely cut off from having contact with any old friends, I was entirely dependent on the whim of my husband; he had become my jailer, the home I had yearned for was now my prison. The only place he took me was to the local pub. It was our habit to go out to dinner each week with the kids. We would go to the pub and eat in the bistro.

"You know what I want," my husband would bark before walking off to the other room where the poker machines were lined up.

My job was to order dinner for everyone. His meal was always the same; sausages, mash, and vegetables - there was nothing adventurous about his eating habits. I would then sit quietly with the children waiting for dinner to be delivered to our table.

Once the meals arrived, my role was to call his mobile phone to let him know dinner was served. Joining us in the bistro he would scoff down his meal with the manners of a ravenous pig before heading straight back to the pokies.

The kids and I would eat our dinner; I tried to maintain a semblance of normalcy, but there was nothing normal about having to sit in a pub bistro for a few hours until their father had finished gambling away, often $400 to $500 a session, on the pokies. The only way he would stop was when his money had run out.

Whenever my husband was near me while we were out, I was on tenterhooks and needed to be cautious with how I spoke, behaved or reacted.

If I said or did something that he felt was inappropriate or offended his code of how he felt I should act, he would grab my hand and squeeze it hard. Once we were back in the privacy of our home and safely behind closed doors away from prying eyes, I would cop a beating because I had dared to open my mouth. I was not allowed to have my own opinion or voice.

When he was driving, I had to sit silently in the front seat next to him. If I made the mistake of speaking, his left hand would, like a flash of lightning, lift from the steering wheel and fly across to strike me across the face. I soon learnt to keep my mouth shut. It has taken many years for me to move past this trauma and become comfortable talking in a car.

The one thing I was allowed to do was open a small craft shop. Because the blind pension is not means tested, I could earn money without it affecting my pension, but the money had to be handed over each night, and every penny accounted for. If I had been doing the grocery shopping, I might have been able to slowly put together a secret fund, but he did the grocery shopping.

His explanation and reasoning for not taking me shopping was that it was far quicker for him to do it alone. If I went with him, then we would need to take the children, so rather than spend time getting the kids and me into the car, it was more efficient for him to do it alone. Incredibly, it made sense to me at the time. Now, I look back and see this was about controlling me rather than being a practical solution.

A chain smoker, smoking rollies of White Ox, marijuana was his breakfast, lunch and dinner washed down with beer. My breakfast was abuse, and every morning hearing "You are fat, you are fucking ugly, and nobody is ever going to want you."

Living in fear of being late with dinner, I would come home from work and fly around the kitchen to prepare our evening meal as dinner needed to be on the table at 6pm each night along with a cold beer. Sausage, mash potato and vegetables. Sometimes there were rissoles instead of sausages, and occasionally we had spaghetti. I cooked whatever was brought home for me to use. I had no say. Today, I relish trying new dishes, although I now follow a

Keto diet which has helped enormously with my seizures.

The first assault happened because I was running late with dinner; in front of the children, he began slapping me around the kitchen before bodily dragging me across to our bedroom. Flinging me like a rag doll on the bed, he stopped long enough to slam the door shut, remove the doorknob and flick the slide bolt into the locked position before proceeding to violently rape me.

The sound of our oldest son, only about 4 or 5 at the time, hammering with his little fists outside the door, trying to get in as I screamed in fear of my life is a sound that I will never forget.

When his vicious assault was over, I curled up in a ball on the bed as my brute of a husband calmly unlocked the door and left the bedroom. Our land line telephone hung on the wall in the dining room; I could hear him bragging to his friend, Mark. "Fuck yeah, I just raped the misses."

Eventually, getting my sobs under control and knowing I needed to feed the family, I got up and returned to the kitchen to finish cooking. I wanted to maintain a sense of normality for the children. We each acted as if nothing had happened. It was reminiscent of the behaviour I experienced growing up, and yet here I was, an adult woman with my own children, trapped in a vicious circle of abuse. I kept silent.

The cycle continued. Over the years, I was grabbed by the upper arms and thrown against the wall. Knocked to the ground and dragged along the wooden floors by my feet.

The ribs that he broke countless times in his attacks on me mean that my left ribs have, even now, never properly healed and taking deep breaths is a struggle. A scar across my left eyebrow after needing stitches from a good punch is a lasting visible reminder of the life I escaped.

As a child, it was normal for me to witness my drunken father coming home from the pub reeking of beer; the stench of acrid urine filled the air as he walked into the house each evening and plonked himself down on the couch. Pissing his pants was normal. My husband took it a step further. In his drunken state, he would urinate in the wardrobe on my clothes, into a drawer, or against the front door. My stomach churned with disgust, yet I was powerless to do anything to change the situation.

Scrubbing feverishly using a mix of white vinegar and water, I did my best to remove the stench of urine. I knew better than to speak out as it would only result in another belting. It is no surprise that many years later, I was diagnosed with Battered Wife Syndrome (BWS) and Complex Post Traumatic Stress Disorder (CPTSD).

My epilepsy made it easy for excuses to be made on the occasions when I needed to be admitted to the hospital or if anyone asked questions. I had fallen during a fit was the perfect foil for beatings and injuries to be explained away. Dread twisted in my gut when I knew he was coming home. Some nights I would sleep out on the cold concrete floor of the toilet block in the park behind our house. Being enveloped in the dark out in the enormous park felt safer than being in my own house which was no longer a home.

My stomach had become the main target for beatings and a few days after one particularly severe beating I was admitted to hospital where they performed an emergency total hysterectomy. I was 29 years old.

The aggression and behaviour towards me were no different whether he was sober, drunk, or stoned. Twisting and tugging handfuls of my hair, I would be dragged into a position where he would blow the smoke from his bong into my face. I have never smoked in my life, and it is, to this day something I have a strong aversion to.

Without support, I had no coping mechanisms. I just did the same thing day in, and day out. I became an emotionless robot. No matter what I did, it was never good enough. If I wanted to help with something, I always got "No, because all you ever do is get in the way."

Following years of abuse, finally, at age 37, following yet another physical assault, something snapped inside me. I could take it no longer and walked out of the house with nothing except the clothes I was wearing, my cane and mobile phone. I boarded the first bus that came along determined to escape.

Sitting on the bus, my jumbled thoughts together with the sounds of chattering monkeys in my mind were interrupted by the insistent ringing of my mobile phone. It was Barbra, one of my few friends. Barbra's call came out of the blue; she had sensed I needed her support. On hearing I was on a bus going to goodness knows where she persuaded me to allow her to escort me to the police station to lodge a formal complaint against my husband. With her encouragement, I got off the bus at a pre-arranged stop along the route. Barbra, as good as her word, was waiting for me. Hugging me tightly, she escorted me from station to station. It was evening, and although the first two police stations we visited were closed, Barbra insisted we keep going onto the next station.

It was third time lucky. The desk officer listened to my story, took notes and did whatever it is that a front counter police officer is meant to do. My Irish ancestors must have been smiling down on me as I struck gold. Two detectives came out to interview myself and Barbra.

First, they spoke to us together and after repeated reassurances and winning our confidence, we were then taken into separate rooms, and interviewed independently. I now, many years later, understand that although it had been kindly done, the reason we were separated was to corroborate the details of our stories.

Detective Senior Constable Stephen Papandrea guided me to follow him into his office. Once I was seated, he gently invited me to explain what was happening at home. As I started to share my story, he got out of his chair and came over to me. Getting down on one knee, he took my hand as he sang "Release Me" by Wilson Phillips. Keeping a gentle yet firm hold of my hand he sang the entire song as he assured me that he believed me and was going to help me. His phone call to a magistrate got an immediate Apprehended Violence Order (AVO) against my husband. For anyone unfamiliar with an AVO, it is an order designed to protect victims of domestic violence when they are fearful of future violence or threats to their safety.

The next call was to my local police station, requesting officers to meet us at my home address. It would be their role to serve my husband with the AVO paperwork and have him removed from the house. I was in awe at how fast the arrangements were being made.

I had avoided going to my local police as I had been there before, and every other time, they did nothing except call my mother-in-law, who also worked for the police; she would promptly return me to my abusive husband and turn a blind eye to what had happened. I had little faith in the police because of this.

As the police approached the front door of the house, Detective Senior Constable Papandrea urged me to get down low in the police car explaining it was for my own safety, just in case, my husband produced a gun. I fought a sense of rising panic at the detective's words, and yet to my utter surprise and incredulous amazement, everything went to plan. Feeling surreal, watching from the safety of the police car, I saw my husband being removed from the house with strict orders that he could never return to abuse me. The detective stayed for a few hours to help settle me in. I could not believe how simple it had been, it seemed inconceivable that I now had the house exclusively to myself and my children.

No one had or has subsequently ever done anything like this for me. Years later, I got a tattoo to represent and remember my gratitude for the policeman who saved my life. I am positive that if he had not believed me and chosen to take action, I would not be here today. The tattoo is an eye with fingers coming out of it and a single blue tear. It represents the song he sang to me, "Release Me" along with the song "Black Eyes, Blue Tears" by Shania Twain. This tattoo sits above my knee in a position where anytime I put my hand on my lap, my fingers automatically connect with his fingers. It is my reassurance that someone believed in me, that good people exist and come in many guises. My knight in shining armour was a police officer.

With the AVO in place, I finally had control of my own money. I went mad in the local op shop treating myself to floaty soft cotton dresses in eye popping vibrant colours that fed an empty place in my soul.

I was 37 years old, and up until this time had never owned a pair of jeans or been able to choose my own clothes. A glimmer of light was piercing through into the dark and lonely place deep inside my soul. Even as a kid I rarely had a dress, it was skirts and tops because you got more wear out of them. My new dresses and my first ever pair of jeans represented what I considered to be a final cutting of ties to the past. I had the freedom to be who I wanted to be. From that day forward I have dressed for me.

Each Friday after school, the kids would go to stay with their father for the weekend. I do not believe in withholding access from one parent; it is not fair to the children. Although I did not experience any further physical abuse, thanks to the AVO, his verbal threats against me continued.

"If you ever file for divorce, you're gonna regret it for the rest of your fucking life." He still considered me his property, and I knew that these were not empty threats; they were real. Stalking me, turning up places where I went, I knew he was serious.

Petrified to file for divorce despite desperately wanting to be free of a marriage I should never have entered, I lived under an ominous dark, brooding cloud filled with doom. The cloud hovered relentlessly until one morning when I woke up filled with a sense of purpose.

A wave of calm, steely determination engulfed me. I have no idea where this feeling came from. Flinging back the bedsheets, I jumped out of bed, hastily showered and flung on some clothes before determinedly heading downstairs to the office. Retrieving the divorce application papers from their hiding place tucked under the fax machine, I grabbed them and headed out the door to file my paperwork. I had filled the forms in months earlier but had never had the courage to take the final step.

Waking in the hospital with a broken jaw, and bruised black and blue from head to toe, my first thought was I must have had a seizure. I soon learnt the truth.

The divorce papers had been served; true to his word, my husband had carried out his threat that I would regret trying to divorce him.

He had come to the house and beaten me so severely that I needed hospitalization; he took away our children but at least the Irish gods were on my side; I had survived the beating that was no doubt intended to send me to my grave.

Terrified of being alone, constantly looking over my shoulder my every waking moment was spent living in absolute fear of him coming back to finish the job he had started. My fitful, restless sleep was filled with nightmares. There was no way I could go back to living in the house.

The children were now living with their father and did not want to return to live with me. Ironically, in 2009 I won the 'Mum in a Million' contest after being nominated by my children. The prize was meant for the 'perfect' family for the parents to renew their vows, instead it was won by a single mum. Rather than taking my 'husband' to renew our vows on the Queensland island luxury resort holiday that was the prize, I took my kids on the 'honeymoon' package.

I was the disciplinarian, trying to bring them up to understand boundaries and the need to work for what they wanted. I knew life was hard, had a solid grasp of finances, and I wanted the same for my children. Using a spreadsheet; which I was first introduced to me as a 16-year-old working at the Department of Agriculture - Biological and Chemical Research Institute, we would have a family discussion on the lists of tasks to be done around the home. I was actively encouraging them to work for what they desired by making each chore in the house worth a certain amount of money.

Together we would set the payment value for every task. Each child then had the opportunity to choose the jobs they wanted. Some jobs were worth 20c and others considerably more. At the end of the week, we would tally up the spreadsheet columns, and I would hand over their pay. It was an agreement that they could use their earnings in any way they wanted. If they chose not to do their allocated tasks, there was no pay.

I have always felt strongly that it was important for children to understand how the world works from a financial perspective. Understanding the financial side of the world allows you freedom, a lesson I learnt the hard way. I did not want this repeated in the lives of my own children.

After being whisked away by their father to live where there were no rules, to be in a place where they were given anything they asked for, including a motorbike, they did not want to return to be with me. They had been won over by money.

I did not have either the physical or mental strength to put up a fight, the children were older, and I was running for my own life. I had done the best I could for my family. Resigning myself to the fact that I was on my own, I knew there was only one person to rely on, and that person was myself.

On the run

For my personal safety and peace of mind, I came up with a plan to be homeless. The house, what had been our family home was where all my possessions were. It was fully furnished and standing empty because it was no longer home, it was not, or had it ever been a safe place for me to be. I preferred to take my chances on the street.

Feeling that I would be able to slip more easily under the radar and be less noticeable if I looked sluggish, unkempt and destitute, I went without showering and wore dirty old clothes. I did take my laptop with me; it was my most precious possession that I did not dare leave behind as it served as a lifeline for my research and to aid my memory.

As I gradually made the slow recovery from the injuries sustained as a result of daring to file for divorce, I knew that my first task had to be to find a bank. Somewhere that I could open my own bank account and a place that would handle my money once the divorce was settled.

I owned half a house, and thanks to my husband putting everything in my name to save money, there would be no arguments that I was not entitled to my share. I knew it would be quite a substantial sum of money; there was no mortgage remaining on the property as together we had managed to pay that off and even had an investment property which was where he now lived with the children.

I visited every bank in town which proved to be a real eye opener. Before I even had a chance to open my mouth and speak, I was judged on my appearance. There were eight banks all up.

The range of responses and reactions I experienced ranged from, sorry can't help, we don't have any suitable accounts for you, you don't have the minimum amount to open an account, to please leave.

Each time I left a bank, I would find a place to sit down outside, pull out my laptop and take a few moments to input the information of my experience into a spreadsheet. Recording and documenting the experience in this way was essential as my brain injury made it a challenge for me to remember.

Spreadsheets are my lifeline for keeping a record of what I am doing, when I need to do it, and what the outcomes are. I love the fact that they are so easy to review and that I can adjust the size of the font so I can easily read the entries.

Eventually, at one of the banks, I spoke to a banking officer who was sufficiently trained to understand not to judge someone on appearance alone. I was treated with courtesy despite my appearance, invited to take a seat and share what I was looking for from a bank. She listened without interruption as I explained that I had no money but wanted to open an account for when my Centrelink payments started. Mind you, I was already receiving payments, but she did not need to know that just yet.

"Do you think you will be able to deposit $1 a month when your Centrelink payment starts?" was the first question she asked when I finished my explanation. In response to my affirmative nodding that I should be able to manage that, her next words were, "Let's open an account for you then."

I thought, "Wow! Someone who can see beyond my physical appearance and actually views me as a person."

Blown away by her positive service, I immediately opened an account. The process was not without its challenges as I did not have the identification most people take for granted, but thanks to the supportive staff who went out of their way to help, I was able to open an account.

Opening my account with a $5 deposit, I explained that I would have my divorce settlement funds coming through. "I can't afford for there to be any hiccups as I will no longer be in Australia to sort anything out. It is absolutely imperative there are no hitches."

The teller, understanding my anxiety, excused herself for a moment and when she returned had the bank manager with her. The manager reiterated all that I had been told, repeatedly reassured me and added his personal guarantee that everything would be looked after.

"You have no need to worry," were his final words. I left that bank feeling confident and secure in the knowledge that at last I was getting my financial future on track. I am still with this bank today as I have a strong belief in good customer service, and they provided it in spades. Most important of all, they were there for me when no one else was prepared to even give me the time of day to find out what I needed.

My next mission was to find a travel agent who would help me get out of the country. I was living in Western Sydney so went to Westfield Parramatta and visited every travel agent that was in the area; there were a surprisingly large number of them. Once again it was a similar story to what I had experienced in my search for a bank.

"Look, I don't have any money right now to book a fare. But I need to get out of here. I need help to do something."

"Sorry can't help," or "You won't have enough money," were the common phrases thrown at me. Occasionally, pamphlets were thrust into my hands as they attempted to bundle me out of the door as fast as they could. I took that as a polite way to say, "Piss off. We're not interested in helping you."

My whole body ached, and despite the searing pain in my legs caused by too much walking in one day, I persisted with my quest. The pain was no stranger to me; I had endured far worse. The motivation that kept me going was fear coupled with the knowledge that I was finally in control of my destiny. I pushed on until I finally hit the jackpot when I came across a sympathetic agent, Vanessa, who, just like the teller in the bank, asked me to sit down

"I think I have the perfect idea for you." She then asked me how much I would be able to save. "Have you ever been on a cruise? Cruises are the way to go." Reaching for a brochure, she opened it to a page with prices, "You look in this book and whatever price it says there is the price you pay. It covers accommodation, entertainment, three meals a day and transport." I am sure my eyes were popping out of my head as I took in the wonderful value as she continued explaining, "All you have to pay for is alcohol and any little gifts, you know, or treatments if you want a facial or something like that."

We looked at the cruise brochure together, and by feigning not to have my glasses, she read out the prices to me. On the spot, I signed up for a seven-night cruise from Sydney to New Caledonia and Vanuatu. I left that travel agency with confidence that everything would be ok. I thoroughly enjoyed my short cruise. Vanessa was right. Cruising was a fun and cost-effective way to travel.

Feeling comfortable and confident that Vanessa would understand my true reason for needing to travel, I went back to see her explaining, "I have to get out of Australia for personal safety reasons." I shared with this understanding woman that I lived in fear for my life. I stressed that my first stop had to be Ireland as I needed to go home. We chatted for hours, and I confided my issues regarding my blindness and epilepsy. Without skipping a beat, she began organizing my flights and tours across the world.

I planned to explore some countries on my own, but once it came to places like Egypt, Morocco, and Dubai, I took the advice Vanessa offered "You are a lot better off being on tour than being on your own for safety reasons."

The fear of returning to the house was still with me. I continued being homeless with minimal possessions. By this time, I had discovered a few hacks for living on the street. I learnt that paying for admission into the public swimming pools meant I could have a hot shower on a regular basis and wash my clothes. Returning to my homeless camp under the bridge, I would then string out my travel clothesline, you know, the ones with the little bits of elastic that you twist your clothes through and hang my laundry out to dry.

To save money, I ate what I could forage from the dumpsters at the big supermarkets; items that were at their use by date were perfectly edible. My needs were simple. To eat a little so I did not starve, and most importantly, to get out of Australia so I could stay alive. Fear was my constant companion.

I sold everything that was in my house, literally everything. Taking a picture with my phone, I would load the item and advertise on Gumtree because that was free; then, if it did not sell eBay was my next stop.

When it came time for me to leave Australia, whatever was not sold, I advertised as free for anyone who wanted to come and collect it. Plenty of women came from women's shelters which pleased me enormously to know the items were going to the needy.

Opening the linen closet, I waved my hand, "You can take all the sheets, pillowcases, the towels; you can take whatever you want. It's all free." It was cheaper for me to give it away than to dump it. I got rid of absolutely everything.

Through my tight scrimping and saving, I quickly managed to save enough money from my pension to pay for my first flight from Sydney to Dublin. Vanessa, my trusted travel agent, knew that once my settlement went through, my travel adventure would be paid for in full.

The sale of the house was taking longer than expected as my husband was being obstructive. The courts stepped in because my husband, determined to block me at every turn, was being unreasonable with his expectation of the sale price for the home. He was knocking back every single offer received until the court intervened, stating that if a reasonable offer was made and I agreed to it, the house had to be sold.

I arranged a Power of Attorney so my best friend could act on my behalf and sign all the necessary legal documents whilst I was at the opposite end of the world. I was in the UK when the settlement finally came through.

Travelling the World

I ran from my abusive father and then from my abusive husband. I ran from Australia in fear for my life. All I took with me was my laptop, a pair of long pants, one dress, a blouse, and a couple of pairs of knickers.

I kept on running from country to country, a total of 42 countries, believing that the only way I could be safe was to keep moving. If I kept on the move, there would be less chance of anyone catching up with me. To feel safe, I needed to be far away from Australia, surrounded by crowds of people who did not know me. I was not afraid to be in a crowd. It was being alone that terrified me.

As the plane began its descent into Dublin, my tummy filled with butterflies. My exhausting journey was coming to an end, and I was about to embark on a discovery voyage into the unknown on the other side of the world. Feeling the bump of the aircraft wheels touching down on the runway, the thought flashed through my head, would Ireland be all I expected, or had I pinned my hopes on a fairy tale place that would disappoint me? I was soon to find out.

Once the fasten seatbelt light was extinguished, it was time to grab my bag with its meagre collection of my possessions and disembark to start the new adventure awaiting me. Going through passport control, past the family groups travelling together and waiting at the baggage carousel, I excitedly made my way out of the terminal and across to the airport transfer bus that would transport me to my pre-booked accommodation.

The feeling of welcome relief that engulfed me as I stood on Irish soil for the first time is something I do not have the words to describe. It was as though a weight that I was unaware I was even carrying had been lifted.

Sitting on the airport bus, listening to the chattering voices and conversations of the other passengers, many of whom were returning home from a holiday, I experienced an inexplicable strong emotional wave of love flow through my entire body. Love for the lush green land with its castles, remarkable history, and soft lilting accents that were so totally different from the Australian accent that I was familiar with. A sense of coming home settled into my heart. This was the land of my birth.

After 33 hours of travel, it was a blissful relief to stumble into the shower before climbing into my bed. I was asleep before my head hit the pillow. I had booked a multi-occupant dorm room for a couple of reasons. The first being that I was on a budget, but the most important reason was that I was afraid to be alone. Even now, many years later, I will still choose a shared hostel room if I am travelling alone.

I feel safer when I am surrounded by a crowd of people. Hostels, with their shared multi-dorm rooms, give me a sense of security knowing other people are around. It is when I am alone, especially with a male, that I feel frightened. This is the opposite of many tourists who prefer to have their own rooms and only share when they absolutely must.

Being in a dorm room meant backpacks were dumped everywhere, it was dangerous, but I had trained myself to always look down. I prefer to walk into a low-hanging light rather than trip over something on the floor. At worst, people think I have little confidence because I am looking down. The truth is that this is a safety mechanism for me.

The magnetic pull to visit Ireland coursed strongly through my veins. Dublin was a total contrast to Sydney, where I had been brought up; it lived up to my expectations and then some. There are many historic places to visit in Dublin, a plethora of museums and fascinating tales of days gone by. Exploring on foot and by bus, I was drawn to St Stephen's Green Park, a peaceful oasis of greenery right in the heart of the city.

The park was a delightful surprise brimming with history; the biggest thrill was learning of a special area in the northwest corner where a garden had been planted especially for the blind. As soon as I stepped into this magical space, the scent from the plants tickled my nostrils, inhaling deeper I touched the plants, which I later learnt were specially chosen so people like me, those who are legally blind, can indulge our sense of touch and smell which are more highly developed than in those who have full vision.

The plants, labelled in braille, which I cannot read due to losing the sensation of the ability to 'feel' as a result of my brain surgery, make the garden layout centred around a seat close to the fountain dedicated to commemorating the memory of suffragist Louie Bennett who founded the Irish Women's Suffrage Federation a restful, must visit spot in Dublin for those without their sight.

Choosing not to visit the place I was born was a deliberate decision. Prior to travelling to Ireland, I had decided not to attempt to find out anything about my birth mother. It may sound weird to others who are adopted and crave to know their history, but something inside me was warning me to leave the past behind, to leave it alone.

The circumstances of my birth were a dark chapter in Irish history; records were difficult to come by and, in many cases, had been destroyed. It was my choice to focus on moving forward with my life. What had happened to me was in the past; this was my time for rebirth and the start of a new life of freedom. I did not want to start digging up any skeletons, given the progress I had made both physically and mentally since I had recuperated from the physical attack that followed my filing for divorce.

My immediate concern now was to stay safe, hidden and far away from where my husband might ever find me. I lived in fear that he might somehow locate me and knew full well that if he did, this time, I would not be lucky enough to survive. By keeping moving, I could stay safe.

Ennis, the Gaelic Medieval town in County Clair, is the place I was drawn to. I do not know why this 6000-year-old town held such an attraction for me, but I was drawn like a magnet to the town and the people.

The slogan for Ennis is "Old Town, New Stories", and that was also exactly me. I was the old Janice in years but with a new story beginning. It was a time of rebirthing for my soul.

Completely at home navigating the narrow main streets, a labyrinth of laneways and bow-ways, I never got lost and instinctively knew which direction I needed to head. It was as though I had lived here in a past life, I ended up spending several months living in Ennis.

Vanessa had arranged my itinerary to be flexible, so although I had forward bookings, I could travel when I felt the need to move on. A hop on, hop off bus tour around Europe, with BusAbout, including Morocco meant that I had transport covered, and in the different cities, I booked individual additional tours as the whim took me.

The group I travelled with were quite a bit younger than me; I was the late bloomer, closer to 40 than 30, and yet, until the moment I started to travel, I had never really lived; I had existed. All my travel companions wanted to do was drink and party, which worked to my advantage as they were not quite as in tune with my disability making it easier for me to keep my secret.

My mini guide, which fits into the palm of my hand, was my lifeline. The small, discrete device with its wrist strap was my essential accessory to help me navigate my way across the world. Neither the tour guides nor my fellow travellers ever cottoned on to the fact that I was legally blind.

Recommended to me by Guide Dogs NSW, where I got my first cane, I was one of the first people trained to use the Miniguide when it was introduced. The guide was supposed to supplement the use of my cane, but I have managed to master using it without the cane.

It looks a bit like a torch or a voice recorder to the casual onlooker, which made it so easy to carry about without drawing attention to myself. Using ultrasonic echo location to detect objects the guide vibrates to warn me of the distance to objects. There are different detection ranges that can be set from 1.5 feet to 24 feet, depending on the environment and skill level of the user; I've become highly skilled over the years. The faster the vibration, the closer the object is.

Using the guide, I can be alerted to doorways, trees, lamp posts, people, and unexpected obstacles like cars and even stairs. It keeps me safe, and I have become extremely adept at using it.

The biggest challenge I faced on my travels was a bicycle tour in Poland; it was a group excursion through town, and I had not fully comprehended that this tour would mean I would need to ride an actual bicycle! I was not sure that I would be able to manage this planned trip. The guide encouraged me to get on the bike, even after I explained that the last time I had ridden a bicycle was as a child, and that was more than 20 years ago!

"Riding a bike is something you never forget," were the group's reassurances.

"Ah yes, but you lot don't know I am blind," was the answer on the tip of my tongue.

The only way out of this was to confess my blindness or get on the bike. Throwing caution to the wind, I clambered astride my bicycle, one of my hands resting normally on the bike with the other one, clutching my mini-guide more upright and hanging on for dear life as my feet worked the pedals.

I rode at the back of the pack and managed to stay with the group successfully without running into anyone or falling off. A sense of exhilaration and relief surged through me as we returned our bicycles at the end of the tour; thankfully, I did no harm to myself or anyone else in the group. I felt pretty invincible!

I never set out to discover myself. I travelled because I needed to run. I lived in fear of being found, and with social media and the technology we have available today, it is easy to find people when you decide to really look.

As I moved like a nomad from country to country, a total of 42 countries, with only a backpack and my laptop, I began to find myself as a person.

The real Janice, who had been suppressed for so long, burst forth into life. I was like the houseplant who had been left in the corner to wilt and die, never watered yet hanging onto life by a slender thread. As the water started to hit my limp leaves and flow down to my roots, I found strength. The strength to move myself to a place where I could eventually become whole. I slowly emerged, coming out of my shell and learnt a lot about myself. I enjoyed finding out what I could and could not do.

I came to understand that success really does lie on the other side of fear and that sometimes, you just have to follow your gut, even when it does not make complete sense or sound logical. I also did some really dumb things along the way!

Visiting Turkey for the second time, I stayed with a community. They took me to a massive, and I mean massive, waterfall. The crescendo of the power of the water thundering over the falls told me that this was one ginormous body of water. Two of the guys led me behind the fall – they go there every day, so know exactly what they are doing – guiding me to the edge, they sat me down before letting go.

Screaming my head off in a combination of fear and exhilaration the water pummelled my body whilst carrying me down the rock surface that was hard, unforgiving and not entirely smooth. I skinned my bum but had so much fun! I was laughing so hard, and now, when I think back all I can say is thank goodness I was not tattooed at that stage because I would have lost half of the artwork.

Memories of Morocco will stay with me forever, the looks of puzzlement on the faces of the children as they curiously touched my tattooed skin, and their shrieks of amazement as they struggled to understand how it was 'real' and not painted on like a henna that eventually wears off.

While enjoying a meal with my tour group, a group of local women gathered around our table and, with the encouragement of our tour guide, ushered me into a back room. I did not understand what was going on and because I could not see, was unsure of what was happening, but everyone was laughing and giggling, so I went along with the occasion.

Gentle hands urged me into different clothing, helping smooth the dress down my body before turning to work on my hair. Tinkling musical laughter and giggles filled the air as one brushed through my red locks while the others tittered away in Arabic. Although I could not understand a word, I presume it was my pale white skin and flame-red hair, a total contrast to their own skin and dark hair, that was the subject of discussion as they spent so much time touching my skin and stroking my hair.

Once the ladies were finished, I was lifted onto an *amaria* - an intricate roofed platform - carried by 4 to 6 men into the restaurant. I felt like a princess sitting in the center of the platform as the procession of bearers swayed through the restaurant to the resounding cheers of the patrons. Smiling and waving at the blurry figures in front of me, I basked in the moment of being the center of attention for all the right reasons; being cheered on was a new experience for me. I was more familiar with being the recipient of harsh words, verbal and physical abuse. The cheers were a balm to my needy soul.

    It turned out I was being carried towards my groom, a man who had actively pursued me on our bus tour and whom I had gone to great lengths to avoid being alone with. The thought flickered through my mind that, hopefully, none of this was real, and it would turn out to be a joke. Being with a crowd of people from my tour made me feel safe, although being the bride in a fake marriage ceremony took me by complete surprise.

    A traditional Moroccan wedding happens over 3 days, and the actual legal marriage takes place before the celebrations. What transpired in the restaurant was a re-enactment of Day 3 of a traditional wedding. My collection of photographs is a lasting reminder of an occasion that further validated that I was attractive enough to be chosen to be treated like a princess. I was the star of the show and felt a million dollars. It was all an elaborate joke designed by our tour guide to add to the memories of our adventures in Morocco.

Festivals formed a big part of my travel plans. They offered a way to experience local cultures, and right to the present day, with parkruns, I choose my runs to coincide with what is happening in the area. Festivals are joyous occasions with large crowds of people, which for me represent safety and fun; two things that I have always craved.

Seeing and learning about local culture feeds my appetite for knowledge. I am always game to try the local food and drinks and never turn my nose up at anything offered as, after all, I am in a different place where there is a need to respect different traditions, customs, cultures, and food.

Part of immersing myself in local culture meant enjoying several steins at the largest folk festival in the world, the Octoberfest celebration in Munich, Germany. A marvel of sound, sights and smells with magnificent parades, costumes and celebrations of Bavarian heritage that went beyond beer. It was here that I was proposed to by a young British army officer.

We had met earlier on my European adventures; he was young, handsome, and probably slightly tipsy when he pulled off the flip tab of a can of coke and held it out to me as an engagement ring. His proposal brought back those vile words my husband used to fling at me, "You're fat, you're ugly and no one is going to want you."

I knew once my divorce came through that I would never get married again. Maybe this proposal was in jest but, all the same, it brought a lump to my throat as I realised that here was a man with everything in front of him that wanted me – blind Janice with half a brain was actually attractive to another man. A man that was younger, more dashing and infinitely better looking than my monster of a husband had ever been. I said no, of course, but it is a powerful memory that sticks with me, a reminder that my husband was wrong.

La Tomatina, in Buñol, Spain would have to be my favourite festival. Imagine being able to chuck tomatoes at each other with no repercussions?! This unique festival, which has been held annually since 1945, actually began when a group of boys made a boy trip up; he got so mad he began chucking things about. A mini riot started with tomatoes from a vegetable stall being grabbed by the crowds to pelt each other with.

The other version of the story goes that it is a celebration of the town patron saint, San Luis Bertrán, and the Virgin Mary. Whichever way you look at this, it comes down to being a giant food fight which sounded like great fun.

This festival is only open to those over 18 where, unbelievably, the population of the tiny town doubles overnight. Capped at 22,000 participants, I was lucky enough to have been one of them. The event, which only lasted an hour, began with trucks loaded with tomatoes and a group of locals throwing tomatoes at the throng of festivalgoers.

The cannon fires to signify the start of the festival; everyone starts scrambling to arm themselves with red projectiles.

According to the rules of La Tomatina, the tomatoes must be squashed before they are hurled, but not everyone follows the rules.

On signing up for La Tomatina you are told that the dress code is old clothes that you are prepared to chuck away, although I had heard that some people choose to wear a white T-shirt, guess it makes them a better target, and the smart ones wear their bathers underneath. My wardrobe was a pair of tomato red shorts, a dark blue singlet top and my bikini underneath.

By the time the cannon fired to signal the end of the fight I was a hot mess that resembled someone who had been dunked in a vat of cooking tomatoes. The soft squishy fruit were in my hair, dripping all down my face, between my boobs, down my cleavage, nestled in my belly button and waist band of my shorts. My white sneakers were stained and remained tinged a pale pink colour despite the scrubbing I gave them.

Well and truly pelted by the tomato-hurling crowd I felt so free. It was pure fun. I felt young, stupid and totally alive as strangers threw tomatoes at me. Call it crazy but the feeling my heart would burst with joy overcame me as I felt the widest of grins spreading across my face as I stood amidst the crowd hurling tomatoes left, right and centre into the throng of people surrounding me. I was behaving like a complete idiot, and no one was telling me I could not do that!

Discovering Myself

"Travel the world and discover yourself," is one of my favourite sayings. It was as I was travelling that I started to fully realise the level of victimization I had experienced.

My entire life, until I decided to run from Australia, had been one lived in fear. It was only once I got away, once I started to travel and be amongst people from different backgrounds, that it began to dawn on me exactly how abnormal the life I had been leading was. Seeing families enjoying carefree times on the beach, watching old couples holding hands, laughing and smiling at each other with open affection as they delighted in being together showed me another side to relationships. These families actually liked each other, the easy open laughter was nothing like I experienced at home.

I had lived my childhood behind a carefully erected façade designed to keep questions at bay. It was years later that my mother in law revealed to me that a policeman who lived in the same street as my family, had mentioned to her that he had often thought something was amiss with our household. And yet, he never bothered to knock on the door to check. Everyone in the neighbourhood had turned a blind eye to what was happening.

The process of discovering myself was not instantaneous; I did not wake up one day with an epiphany. It was a gradual dawning that, day by day, slowly began to illuminate the dark recesses of my mind.

The experiences I had been through were deeply suppressed; it was, I believe a safety mechanism for me, a way to be able to continue to function because the realities of what I went through were too horrendous to contemplate.

It was not just the physical beating and assaults. The verbal tirades, the constant putting down no matter what I did. I had been living in a bubble where the one constant was fear.

Each country I moved through showed me another way of life, and the shutters that had bound me to my insular world began to lift. I began, without consciously realising what was happening; to redefine myself, gradually creating a new sense of self and self-worth.

Where other people buy a souvenir as they travel, I get tattooed. There is no excess baggage to check in, no need to find room in your luggage or security check because it's an odd shape. A tattoo is much easier, and I have already got enough baggage for a lifetime and then some!

I was very angry when I got my first one. I could not believe the relief I felt once I had the tattoo. It felt like all the pain was taken away. It gave me hope. This feeling lasted for six months straight. It was the best six months of my life.

The pain started to return. I went and got another tattoo. I realised getting inked was therapeutic. To me, it was serious therapy.

I came to the conclusion that paying for a tattoo, although a lot dearer than many souvenirs, was definitely the way to go for me. My souvenirs are with me for a lifetime without the risk of being broken, lost or forgotten.

The fascinating 17th-century city of Amsterdam, with its progressive, vibrant and tolerant attitude towards individuals, is where I discovered a private Tattoo Museum.

Being on my own in the cyclist's capital of the world did not stop me from getting on out to join the street party for Queen's Day. Choosing not to take my chances on a bicycle, I stuck to walking as my mode of transport.

I became friends with two street musicians. One was wearing a bright green suit, and the other was wearing a bright orange suit. I could not take my eyes off them. Unsure if the attraction was because they were wearing bright colours, which meant I could easily spot them or whether it was that they were wearing the colours of Ireland; maybe it was a bit of both, and either way, they were awesome.

The tattoo museum was an eye opener with the tattooed skin hanging on the walls plus a full tattooed body of a deceased individual on display which absolutely captivated me. I delved further into this fascinating display with the owner and even went as far as to sign paperwork for my body to be on display when my time was up. I arranged that my body was to be skinned and hung on display in the museum, and then the rest of me should be sent to Ireland to be cremated. My ashes would then be scattered over St. Stephen's Green. Unfortunately, this museum closed in 2013, which means my plans to be skinned are thwarted. It is still my intention to be cremated and scattered at St Stephen's Green in Dublin. My desires are clearly written in my will, and it will be up to my executors to find a way to make this possible.

In Jerusalem, as I was waiting in the lobby for the guide to turn up for the Holy Land Tour that I had booked, an elderly couple walked in. I could immediately see they were uncomfortable with my presence. In their nervousness, the gentleman dropped his walking stick, and as he bent slowly and shakily to retrieve it, I stepped forward, "I'll get it for you."

"Thank you. We were so scared because you look very rough and criminal," blurted his wife as I held out the walking stick. I had a few tattoos, and I am sure that it was my tattoos that had sparked this reaction in them. I did ponder whether they were Jewish and had perhaps lived through the Holocaust.

"Well, I am everything but that." I responded with a smile before walking away to another area of the lobby as I never like to make anyone feel uncomfortable and figured putting some distance between us would allow them to be more relaxed.

Eventually, the tour guide arrived. The elderly couple were on the same tour; the 3 of us boarded the bus to join our travel companions for the day. There were 12 of us in total, all middle-aged Americans except the elderly couple who, it turned out, were Canadian, and then there was me! Bright red hair, colourful body and legally blind Janice, who was travelling alone and stuck out like a sore thumb.

As the day went on, the elderly couple needed assistance getting on and off the bus, up and down the stairs etc. Nobody in our group, not even the tour guide, offered to assist, except for me. It did strike me as ironic that the person who had the least vision was the one helping.

When we reached Masada, the only way to get decent photographs of the unique site was to walk up hundreds of stairs to the top. "Would you like me to take your camera and get some photos? You can then brag to all your friends that you climbed up to the top to get the best photos." I had my mini-guide which gave me the confidence I could tackle the steps.

Accepting my offer, the realisation dawned on the elderly Canadian couple that I was simply an ordinary genuine person who loved to travel and was happy to assist fellow travellers as necessary.

My day out into the Judean Desert made me think deeply about the resilience of the human spirit that Masada, a UNESCO World Heritage site, represents as not only a symbol of Jewish cultural identity but also of the continuing human struggle between oppression and liberty.

The reality of the Dead Sea outstripped all the stories I had been told. Stepping into the water felt distinctly weird, tiny nicks and cuts I had not known I had started to sting the moment the water came into contact with my body. I learnt it was the extremely high concentration of dissolved mineral salts in the water that made it denser. As our body weight is lighter than the density of the water, our bodies are more buoyant in the Dead Sea. Floating easily in this ancient body of water that stems back to biblical times, I made sure to follow the advice of our guide and kept my mouth shut; I did not accidentally want to swallow any of the salty water.

It was almost impossible to stand and connect with the bottom as my feet kept being pushed up; I was walking on water!

Baptised in the Church of England, although my family never took me to church, I am not particularly religious, but that moment felt like a miracle; I was in Israel, floating in the Dead Sea. I was alive and far removed from my abusers.

Returning to Australia

On hearing the news that I had a grandchild, the dye was cast, and I decided it was finally time to return to Australia. For so long, I had yearned to have a family of my own; even though it had not worked out with my own children, a grandchild was a new life, another opportunity and I did not want to let that pass. I needed to return to Sydney.

Tory, my lovely gay friend, who I had met on a float at the Sydney Gay and Lesbian Mardi Gras, stood waving madly and calling out my name as I walked out of the international arrivals at Sydney Airport. I feel safer and more comfortable with gay men because I know they are not interested in me as a woman. We had kept in touch while I was on my travels, and on hearing I was returning to Australia, Tory, in his typically kind fashion, invited me to crash on his couch while I regrouped and decided what my next move was going to be.

The value of a cruise made it a no brainer for me to decide to invite my friends and family to come on a cruise as part of our reunion. The cruise was out of the port of Brisbane, it was to be my treat, and I would cover all the expenses for cabins and meals. I had continued to live frugally despite having the settlement from my divorce, plus I maintained my habit of staying in hostels on my travels; using some of my money to treat family and close friends felt like the right thing for me to do.

My hope was that it would give us a chance to rebuild relationships and yet have the privacy that I was certain we would need as we worked on getting to know each other again. There was a lot of history to cover, and I was sure there would be many questions that the time at sea together would allow us to explore.

"Who the fuck are you?" were the first words out of Barbra's mouth as she looked me up and down. This was the woman who had insisted on taking me to the police station that fateful night where I had managed to get away from my husband.

"And what have you done with Janice?" The look of incredulity on her face as she took in my newly found persona was priceless.

"Janice is too shy." Barbra could not stop staring at me. "She wouldn't look at anyone's face. She always looked down. You are not Janice! What have you done with her?"

"This is the new me," I proudly announced with the biggest grin spread across my face as I sensed them all gawping at me in amazement. I had knocked their socks off with my new confidence and colourful body art. It was at moments like this that I really wished I was able to see their expressions which, I have no doubt, would have been priceless.

Once our cruise was over, it was time to think about settling back in Australia again. I wanted to have the security of a place that I could call my own home. Somewhere that held no history and where I could feel safe living alone. I had the money from my divorce settlement and my blind pension plus zero interest in any kind of relationship. I knew that I would be single forever.

Newcastle was being talked about as being an affordable city that was not too far from Sydney. Tory, as it happened, was headed to Newcastle for a blind date with a chap he had met online. "You come on up with me," he invited.

"Yeah, like, I'm gonna go on a date with you two."

"Don't be stupid," he laughed. "We'll go to Newcastle together and get a room for a couple of nights. We'll get pissed on Friday night. I'll meet up with him on Saturday. You can have a look around. Then we get pissed again on Saturday night. And we come home Sunday."

When he put it like that, it sounded like a reasonable plan. I agreed to go along and while there would look at properties. I had already decided that a studio would best suit my needs; the bigger the place was, the more rooms there were, the more housework and cleaning would need to be done. I wanted a studio within walking distance of everything – the train, the shops, the pub. I walked around Newcastle for the entire Saturday while Tory was on his date. I liked what I saw, so much so that a week later, I caught the train back up for a better look.

I looked up a real estate agent, called and explained what I was looking to purchase. The agent showed me three units, two of them in the same block. The third was actually on Beaumont Street, where all the restaurants, cafes, and pubs are located.

"I'll take number 8," I announced to the surprised real estate agent and signed the papers on the spot. The studio I chose was on Maitland Road, only 3 metres away from Beaumont Street.

It was on the top floor, and there was no lift. It was the perfect location for me; amongst the many things that I had been told, along with the fact I was not likely to live beyond 25, was that I'd never be able to walk upstairs again. The location of the studio meant I needed to walk up and down the stairs every day. This would provide more challenges for me, but I am used to a challenge. You could say that I thrive on a challenge. Tell me I cannot do something and watch me do my uttermost to succeed.

Where does the expression life begins at 40 come from?! I used to hear it frequently, which never made any sense to me. I could not understand what the significance of 40 was. How could it be different from any other year? What makes 40 more special than 30 or 50? I used to think, "That sounds so stupid."

Celebrating my 40th birthday on St Patrick's Day at the Irish pub, PJ Gallaghers Hotel at Parramatta meant free Irish entertainment. As someone who loves music, and especially Irish music, I was in my element kicking up my heels and downing a few wee drams of Irish whiskey to mark the year that life was meant to begin.

It was during these celebrations that an epiphany hit me "Oh, my God, my kids are grown up. I'm happily divorced. I'm a free woman. I can go where I want, do what I want."

Life had begun. I finally understood what was meant by life begins at 40. It all started to make sense. I was married at 23, left my husband at 37 and was divorced at 39. It was true, life does begin at 40!

I did Google and discovered that the phrase was adopted after an American author, Walter B Pitkin released a self-help book in 1932 titled "Life Begins at 40." Interestingly, this was the era when the population was starting to experience longevity of lifespan.

It turns out that one piece of advice given in Pitkin's self-help book is that once you hit 40 you should look at leading a simplified life and reduce parenting to a minimum. The irony of the phrase and his advice is not lost on me. I am blessed to have seen my 40th birthday despite being told, by medical experts, at 19 that it was neigh on impossible for me to survive beyond 25. I had well and truly proved them wrong.

My life became simplified once I turned 40. I had learnt to speak up and make my wishes and opinions heard. Instead of allowing others to tell me what I could and could not do, I had become empowered. The meek and mild Janice no longer existed; in her place was Janice that roars.

Inwardly I might be quaking, and I am still afraid to be alone. I do not like upsetting people, and struggle to tell anyone that I am unhappy with their actions, yet on the outside, I appear strong and speak up for myself.

My Body, My Canvas

It was after making a move from Sydney and settling into Newcastle that the next stage of my life took off. I was with a couple of friends at Cardiff RSL; we had been for dinner and to see a band that was playing; it was a fundraising night for breast cancer. We were sitting chatting when a woman stopped by our table,

"I want to shoot you!" A frisson of fear shot up my spine at her words. I went into panic mode, a look of pure terror on my face which prompted her to hurriedly say, "Oh No! I mean I want to photograph you".

"Why? I'm old. I'm fat. There's nothing special about me."

"You've got a lot," she replied, "You've got a lot to show." And it was at that point I understood it was my tattoos that caught her eye, as by now, I'd got to the stage where I was brave enough to show my colourful body off.

I had no idea that you could be a tattoo model. I agreed to do a shoot with her and really enjoyed it. She was easy to get along with and I even got paid. Modelling for her gave me a taste of freedom and attention that I had not previously known.

That was the beginning of my modelling career, a chance meeting in a pub. I set up a Facebook page with some photos of myself from the shoots and people started following me. A few months later, I was tagged in a Facebook post. A company in Sydney was looking for models. Clicking on the post, I attached a full body nude from a previous photo shoot and, before I could reconsider, quickly pressed send to the address given on the post. Liking what they saw, the producers invited me to a casting interview.

Travelling on the train from Newcastle to Sydney for work, commuters would openly stare.

"Go get a job ya dole bludger."

Others would shift uncomfortably and visibly move a distance away from me. My tattooed appearance caused people to make assumptions; I was not working, had a criminal record, was a druggie or something equally sinister and unsavoury.

I remember a particular time living in Newcastle. I was on the morning train, dressed in shorts, a singlet top, and pair of thongs because that was the uniform for my work role, travelling to Sydney, where I was filming. The train was packed with commuters going to work just like myself. A woman walked up and shouted directly into my face, "Are you a fucking junkie? Why don't you get a job?"

She was making assumptions based on my tattoos that I was a junkie. It hurt because I was just like every other commuter on that train. I was on my way to work. The point of difference between us was they were wearing suits or uniforms that fit into what the general population saw as appropriate work wear. Technically, I was wearing my uniform too.

The reality of my life was so far removed from the preconceived prejudice of most of the public. Magazine covers, television series, movie roles and advertising campaigns surrounded by photographers, producers and household name stars were my new life. As with all industries, there is an award rate; when it comes to modelling, the award covers fully clothed, lingerie and nude modelling. As a fully tattooed model, I was in demand, with most of the work being nude shots.

Doing nude work never bothered me. The heavy tattoo work made it look like I was clothed. Alice Cooper remarked when he met me, "Oh, it looks like somebody splashed paint all over you."

Being so heavily tattooed at a nudist festival, I was once mistaken for being dressed in a body stocking with the security guard telling me I needed to take off my clothes. He did a double take when I explained I was already naked and what he thought was a body suit was colourful, permanent ink decorating my skin.

I decided to work under the professional name of Crystal Waters because I knew that the personal and professional needed to be kept separate; I had learnt about this from a friend who was in the entertainment industry.

I chose the name Crystal to represent purity because although I looked like I was tough, and was cast in stereotypical roles, I am a softie with a pure heart, have never been to jail, except in the movie parts I played and am not at all tough despite what the exterior may suggest. Waters was my married name. Crystal Waters had a nice ring to it. Crystal projected confidence. She was brave, stood up to everyone and could do anything she set her mind to.

Having been diagnosed with Battered Wife Syndrome, when I was cast as a victim of domestic violence, I needed several breaks due to the flashbacks of my personal life. The memories cropped up when least expected and up until that time, I had managed to keep my personal and professional life in two separate compartments.

I agreed to model as a female abuser to promote domestic violence against men. It is important to me to break the stereotypical view that it is only women who are abused. I chose to do this as I am over the community and advertising giving the impression that men are always the abusers and never the victims.

The male model I worked with, Peter, was incredible. I experienced an extraordinary sense of trust and responsibility as he allowed me to get up close and hold a knife against him; especially since he knew my history of domestic violence.

The diversity of my roles has included modelling as a blind woman to show that the blind community are still part of the 'community' and can be just as independent as a sighted person. I also modelled as a mental health patient to demonstrate that this sector of our community needs assistance and treatment rather than isolation and neglect.

On the flip side of this coin, I rejected and knocked back many roles in film, including for household television series, as I was heartsick and offended by being asked to play the role of the abuser or stereotypically cast into being aggressive and punching people out for no reason purely based on my tattooed appearance.

Imagine, a woman who fears being in a room alone with a male or anyone who has a large body frame due to the effects of Battered Wife Syndrome but yet always gets the role of the abuser. My small contribution by refusing to take roles or agreeing to take roles that turn the tables is one way to help break down the barriers. It might not be much, but it all has to begin somewhere as every little action helps to dispel and change perceptions, albeit slower than I would like.

What had started as a personal outlet for pent-up emotional anger had become a means for me to earn a livelihood. I memorialize occasions and locations with a tattoo. Every tattoo on my body has a meaning that is deeply personal.

When I decided to write this book, I never intended to share the story behind my tattoos, but a little voice started whispering in my ear, "Janice, it's time to share."

On each occasion, I whispered back, "But they are too personal. I'll share what they mean at my funeral."

The bossy voice became louder and more insistent the deeper I got into writing this memoir. "They are part of you...share!!"

I think the voice is actually my conscience, prodding me to spill the beans because it is the question everyone wants to ask when they meet me for the first time. I took out my anger on myself. You know, as I say, it is my body and I'll abuse it as much as I like, but I abuse it with ink rather than drugs. No one is being harmed.

I did not know what to expect when I went for the first tattoo; I had never had one before and suspected there might be a bit of pain involved. It hurt like hell, but I felt relieved at the same time.

People take their anger out in different ways, some by assaulting someone, committing a crime or doing drugs; none of that interests me. Getting tattooed was, for me, like a sort of self-harm, but I was never suicidal at any time. I had no idea how much the tattoos would help me; it was and continues to be so therapeutic. Life, to me, is very much for living to the full, as best I possibly can.

My body is my canvas. My canvas is my history. My history has made me who I am today, split my body in two and every tattoo on the right side of the body is based on abuse that I've experienced. And every tattoo on the left side of my body is based on death that I've experienced. I decide on my own tattoos. The actual design of the tattoo represents the physical side of the story.

The colour is the emotional side to the story. And where it's tattooed on my body is the spiritual side to the story. And then every tattoo on my body, starting from one part of my body going up and down are the lyrics to one song word for word.

What is that song? That is one thing I am keeping private; it will be played at my funeral.

The first tattoo I ever had done is dedicated to the little girl born to an unwed mother in Catholic Ireland. Given up for adoption, diagnosed with epilepsy, abused by her father; this kid had no chance to live a normal childhood. The location choice for my first tattoos was so they could be easily hidden; they were for me, not for public viewing.

The tattoo on my right shoulder is a devil standing over a skull. It is representative of the fact that ever since my brain surgery operation, I've been living in hell. 'Go To Hell' by Alice Cooper is the theme song for this one. I love music and find it soothing, so I assign each of my tattoos a little musical theme.

On my left shoulder sits a laughing skull with a gun. It is representative of my thoughts, 'that the day I laugh is the day I blow your brains out' because that is exactly what the surgeons did to me. I know it is against the law to shoot someone; the tattoo gave me the relief that I was able to show my anger and express myself freely. 'Lock Me Up' again by Alice Cooper is the theme song I associate with this one.

By now, having had my first three tattoos, I understood that the physical act and process of being tattooed was the only way to adequately express all the pent-up rage and anger I had bottled up inside myself without doing physical harm to anybody (except myself).

The tattoo of Alice Cooper on my back represents three of his songs that I can truly relate to, and the positioning is something that people would never understand.

The portrait is black because my entire life has been total darkness from day one. This represents the song I'll Never Cry (because I am actually not able to cry or show emotions as most people do).

The text at the bottom reads Take It Like A Woman representing the song title, and the dripping blood symbolizes Only Women Bleed. Both songs are about domestic violence. Positioning the writing at the bottom is deliberate; it is as low as any partner could ever go. Domestic violence is not something anyone should ever experience.

This tattoo is on my back because it is in my past. It is behind me and something I never want to see again. The position of Alice's mouth is covered by my bra band while his eyes poke out above any singlet tops I wear. This represents people seeing what goes on but never speaking up about it.

Tattoos have been a very positive outcome in my life. It also opened the doors to discovering the incredible number of prejudices against those who are a little different, be it having a disability, a different skin colour, being gay or needing to use a wheelchair or a Guide Dog. Disability does not mean a lack of intelligence.

Being tattooed does not mean you are a bad person.

The general public, for the most part, tend to see me and judge.

"She's been in and out of jail. She does drugs; she does crime."

It hurts that the world is prejudiced, which is the reason I go to great lengths to shout out the injustices I experience. I also make a point to give compliments and recognition to those who are doing the right thing. I might be inwardly quaking, but I never back away from speaking up when I see an injustice.

Often, especially in pubs, people want to talk about tattoos, which I actually hate, because there is more to me than tattoos, but I know they are visible so it is only natural they might be curious.

The question that irks me the most is, "Which is your favourite tattoo?" I find this one extremely annoying and grit my teeth before responding, "None of them. I love them all equally because I don't discriminate."

"Why would you do that to yourself?" is the other question. Despite having been asked this exact question countless times over the years, I am still amazed at the sheer audacity and rudeness every time I get asked.

Over the years, I have perfected my answer. "I just get a tattoo every time I'm sexually frustrated." They walk away pretty quickly, and this is my way of saying, "Fuck off. It is none of your business."

Do Not Judge

Having recently moved back to Australia and up to Newcastle, I knew hardly anyone. Happy in my own company, I would go down to the pub where one Friday night, I spotted a notice about a bike and tattoo show. I thought I'll go. I got chatting with another woman and mentioned that I was going to the bike and tattoo show the next day. My new friend was up for the trip; we planned to go together.

"I'll just warn you; I'll be getting my gear off." I thought I'd better warn her, "You know, because I'm going to compete in the tattoo show. So, I have to take my top off." I didn't want to shock her.

"I don't care. I'm going for the music," she shot right back at me without batting an eyelid or missing a beat. We headed off the next day together; I didn't know anyone there except her.

My previous experience with a tattoo contest was in New Zealand, where I won a couple of trophies. Yes, I had turned from shy, does not say a word Janice into someone brave enough to enter a tattoo contest and get her clothes off in front of a crowd of strangers.

This contest was different, much bigger in terms of the number of people attending and the categories available to enter. Each entrant was given an entry number, and all the chicks got up on stage, allowing the judges to score the categories, best arm, best leg, best chest, best colour, best all sorts of stuff. I entered a few categories but never expected to win.

Busy talking when they called out the winning number, I missed the announcement. It was not until the judge, in exasperation at the lack of the winner showing up to claim their trophy shouted out across the room. "Hey, Blue Tits, you've won!"

"Oh shit, I think that's me."

Checking my number, sure enough, it was me. I had won Best Female Back, sponsored by Gladiators, who run the Maitland Bike and Hot Rod Show. It was through winning this contest that I first met Head, their President, who presented me with my trophy. I also won the Female Best Chest, and yes, my chest is blue, which is why the judge was calling out for blue tits.

A month later, a friend invited me to listen to his brother's band playing at the Metropolitan Hotel in Maitland. I decided to go along as it was only a short train ride and walk from where I lived. As it happened, another woman at the pub overheard the invitation and offered to drive me as she had also heard how great the band were.

Finding parking in Maitland on the main road is almost impossible, yet there was a parking spot right smack in front of the pub. It was karma, said my new friend.

Dressed for summer, I was wearing a singlet top and shorts. As I put one leg out of the car, a bloke, whose name I was later to learn was Yowie, was having a smoke outside the front door. Eyeing me up and down he stuck his head back inside the pub bellowing to someone inside, "Get over here and meet your stepmother."

All the big bad boys, dressed in their colours, were sitting at the front bar having drinks while the band played out the back. Head, who had presented me with my trophy, was one of them.

The 1% patch and one-percenter term, as a motorcycle club subculture, traces its roots back to 1947 when the American Motorcycle Association (AMA) held a motorcycle rally in Hollister, California. Following the violence that erupted at the event, the AMA stated, "99% of the motorcycling public are law-abiding; there are 1% who are not."

My personal experiences with the 1%er's have shown me that these guys are often misjudged and discriminated against simply because they are different. I was out of my marriage and free, yet I still lived in fear. Weirdly, I was unafraid of these men.

Deep inside me is a little girl who is caught in a woman's body. Petrified of men, fear of the unknown.... Yet one day, I met someone who seemed very different to all other males. He was covered in ink, wore a patched leather vest, he was a bikie, a 1%er. He was a gentleman.

We chatted, we drank, we laughed, and we got to know each other. He took me to his house and laid me on his single bed. Sitting on a chair, he strummed his guitar chair singing

"Amanda", by Don Williams to me. It's a very sweet song. Putting on some Irish music, he then told me that no woman deserves to be treated the way I have been. No hanky panky, nothing sexual.

After a friendly day out, I got a taxi home and thought about what had happened or should I say what didn't happen. Here we have a big bad boy covered in ink, known to the police, who served time in prison but yet he was an absolute gentleman to me. Yowie was the true definition of do not judge a book by its cover. He gave me the ability to start trusting again.

I became very good friends with these guys, and they gave me a nickname, "Avatar" which is tattooed on my neck. I would go to their clubhouse when they had parties. They were all absolute gentlemen despite their fierce exteriors.

They came to trust me just as I trusted them. When the media wanted to do an interview with them for a program, Yowie called me.

"Avatar, we want you there. You know what we are like," I was surprised and flattered as he continued, "you're in front of the camera every day, plus you've got more ink than us." He wanted me there to ensure they got a fair representation and did not fall into the trap of being stereotyped as big, bad bikies.

Ironically, my career as a tattoo model came to an abrupt halt when I was sexually assaulted by a male photographer. The trauma of my past rape and assaults came bursting through to the foreground.

My gossamer thread of confidence was shattered. I could no longer work in front of a camera. The fear had returned with a ferocious force. Despite my paralysing fear, I played a part in bringing this vile man who preyed on innocent women to justice.

I chose to testify in person at his court case. I had the option to give my evidence via a video link-up, but I needed to demonstrate that despite what he had done to me and to so many other women, he was not going to get away with his despicable actions.

I sat rigidly in the stand, my body inwardly quaking with fear, yet I held myself tall and proud as I delivered my evidence. A surge of deep relief coursed through me when I heard he was convicted. Justice had been served.

To mark my 50th birthday, I signed up for The World's Greatest Shave. It was not long after my move to Queensland, and the heat was getting to me. Although my hairdresser had given me an undercut, so when my hair was down, I still looked like a woman.

Under the shower one morning, as the water cascaded over my trademark red locks, I thought, "Fuck it. I'm gonna do the World's Greatest Shave. I'm gonna go the whole hog." My hair had been a standout feature in my modelling career.

I had experienced a shaven head once before when I was living in Sydney. It was after the car accident that everyone except me was able to step out of the car and walk away from.

Although I cannot remember what happened during the accident, I can tell you everything right up until the time of impact. It is weird how what I did two minutes ago totally vanishes from my memory band, but when it comes to certain times of my life, like the 9th of March 2007, I have complete clarity right up to the moment of the accident.

It was a Friday. After finishing

work at my craft shop at lunchtime, I was allowed to have lunch with my friend Brooke now and then. This was one of the occasions that I eagerly looked forward to. A highlight of an otherwise highly controlled calendar.

On this particular day, I decided I would be daring and order something I had never tasted before. A quiche.

Once our lunch was over, and before Brooke and I left the pub, I phoned ahead my order to the local pizza shop. It had become a regular habit for the kids and me to share pizza on a Friday night for our dinner. My husband and I were still together, but he was spending a lot of time living in our investment property and rarely ate with us.

My husband always came to pick me up after my lunch. It was his way of making sure he knew exactly where I was. No one was in the passenger seat. Brooke and I were in the back.

I do not recall anything of the crash. The impact meant I hit my head. Glass had to be cut out of my eyelid, but I am fortunate there was no further damage to my face. I was in and out of a coma for several weeks. When I regained consciousness, every time I would close my eyes, I would see the heads of people circling round right in front of me. I spoke to someone about this, and it was explained as being a flashback of the paramedics and everyone who cut me out of the car. It was the crew who were trying to treat me. I have no recollection of being cut from the car.

Once I had recovered and was as back to normal as was possible for me, I made my way down to the police station and asked to see the photos of the car. I wanted to understand what had happened to me. The entire left passenger side was smashed in as we had been turning right when the other driver, who had been speeding, ran a red light and smashed straight into my door.

A month later, when I was finally sufficiently well enough to be discharged from the hospital, my hair was a mangled mess of red knots. All the time I was in a coma, it had not been brushed; the tangles were so bad that the knots were permanent fixtures.

Finally, seeing no other option, in desperation, I grabbed the clippers and shaved my head. I was bald only momentarily as I allowed my hair to grow back immediately. This time, thirteen years later, would be different.

The decision to shave was entirely my choice. I was in control of making my own decisions. I decided that if I was being shorn, it should be in the name of a charity, and am proud to say I raised $3,000 for the Leukemia Foundation doing the shave that was run on Facebook live to encourage donations.

At that time, my head was the only part of my body that remained tattoo free. Purple Day, 26th March 2020, a mere six days after the World's Greatest Shave, would be the perfect time to continue the tapestry of ink to include my newly shaven head.

Purple Day is marked across the world annually as a day dedicated to raising awareness of epilepsy. It is sometimes called Epilepsy Awareness Day, but I reckon that Purple Day sounds so much better. As an epileptic, I embrace every opportunity to dispel the common myths and fears of this neurological disorder. Being tattooed has changed my life. For the better. Being inked is an expression and extension of my freedom. It seemed fitting to have my head tattooed on a day that aims to raise awareness and reduce the social stigma of a condition that has had such a significantly profound effect on my own life.

It was considerably more difficult than I expected to find a tattooist willing to take on the challenge. I was forced to search high and low to find an experienced artist who was willing to tackle the surgical region of my head. There is no bone and no plate, just skin. I finally located an artist who was confident enough in their own skills to take on the challenge.

Medical professionals and my friends alike all cautioned me that what I was doing was extremely dangerous. They tried to talk me out of it with dire warning that I could be leaving the tattoo studio in a body bag. Yet despite their warnings, something inside of me was urging me to move forward with my goal of finally having the last part of my naked body inked. The sensible part of me took precautions in case their warnings were going to turn out to be correct, and I was making a disastrous decision to sign my own death warrant. I visited the lawyers to update my will and put all my affairs in order.

Despite my meticulous planning and spreadsheet of tasks all ticked off my plans were thwarted on March 25th when COVID-19 saw Australia once again plunged into lockdown. Having built up my courage, made peace with myself and got all my affairs in order, I was devastated not to be able to go ahead as planned.

The tattoo artist reassured me that I would be his first job once business could resume. Three months later, on 26th June 2020, I walked into the tattoo studio not knowing if I would walk out again or if the dire warnings that I was heading to certain death would come to pass.

Despite the danger involved this was something that I needed to do. It was a risk that I was willing to take. I sat in the chair for 8 hours straight. The job was not complete, but it was time to call it a day. I was halfway through the process. The artist was exhausted. I felt like I had been through the wringer and at the same time, exhilarated.

A Celtic cross with a Claddagh ring in the centre adorned the top of my head. The Claddagh is highly significant in Irish culture and has been around since Roman times. When I stop to think about it, I believe I embraced all the symbolism of Ireland because those are the only roots that I have.

The Claddagh is a symbol of friendship, love and loyalty. It is synonymous of what has been missing for so much of my life. The green, white and orange colour embellishments denote the Irish flag whilst the mountains are representative of the obstacles and challenges that I have had to climb over throughout my life to get to where I am today. I am still climbing those mountains.

A path with the green shamrock of Ireland and orange hearts leading up to the Celtic cross framed by the flames on either side ensures that I never stray from my path to remain loyal, true and love life despite what obstacles the universe may choose to litter along my path. The dark purple clouds with lightning strikes represent the seizures I continuously must fight as an epileptic.

Thankfully, over the years that have passed, I have been able to control my seizures to a degree by adopting a keto diet, which I have since discovered was originally developed to aid epileptics.

My research has shown me that the earliest recorded use of keto for epilepsy was in 1911 by two French physicians. In the early 1920s, doctors at Harvard Medical School studied the effects of starvation as a treatment for epilepsy, with them noting that seizure improvement typically occurred after 2–3 days.

There is also an interesting case study of Dr Atkins, famous for developing the Atkins Diet, in 1970. His diet was used on a 7-year-old girl with intractable epilepsy due to a left parietal cortical dysplasia. She used the Atkins diet for a week in order to adjust to the classic keto diet with the result that three days later her seizures had ceased and remained at bay for 3 years.

When I learnt of these studies that were happening around the same time as my own treatments, it did make me wonder what my own life would have been like if I had been offered these kinds of treatments, even if they were still experimental diets, instead of drugs and brain surgery.

Returned home from the tattooist after having half my tattoo design completed, I fell into a sleep of deep relief interspersed with dreams of the work that still needed to be done. A few weeks later I returned to the studio for what the artist had explained to me was the most difficult and dangerous part. The surgical site.

I sat in the chair for 5.5 hours, enduring wave after wave of absolute agony. I honestly did not think I was going to survive, but I could not back out. It was as if a deep elemental force that came from my darkest depths held me glued to the chair. This was something I was driven to have completed. Summoning every ounce of willpower, drawing on every grain of the survival skills gained over the years of physical abuse, I steeled myself to push through the excruciating pain.

In the surgical area are emblazoned the letters NFR meaning Not for Resuscitation. When my time comes, I have no wish to be resuscitated. All the sections with the holes that the doctors drilled into my head are blocked over. There is a song sung by a beautiful man, Ken Casey, who signed my body that goes with this tattoo. 'Never Walk Alone' is the song, and although I have fought these demons on my own my entire life, I know that my tattoos are always 'by my side', and I am never alone. Ken Casey's signature, along with those of the rest of the Dropkick Murphy's band, is tattooed on my body.

Keeping my head shaved is now normal for me. As an epileptic living in Queensland summers, it is much cooler and far more comfortable. During the colder months, which are few, a beanie keeps me warm.

When I look back at the old photographs of myself with the long red hair, a small smile plays across my face; I remember the happy times, the wild adventures, the dangerous challenges, and most of all, the incredible journey of discovery I travelled on the road to becoming whom that little Irish abandoned orphan girl was destined to be.

The freedom I experience today, as Janice Whittle; single, blind, not quite all there in the head, is because of the journey that I have travelled.

Yes, it was not a picture-perfect life, not by any stretch of the imagination, but I have chosen to always embrace love, to look on the brighter side and to know that laughter and love are what make the world go around. I have also learnt that love comes in many forms, and first and foremost, we must learn to have self-love. This is not an easy lesson to learn. For many of us from backgrounds of domestic violence, it becomes a never-ending cycle. A cycle that can leave little opportunity to escape.

I am blessed to have been able to emerge on the other side of the cycle thanks to my own tenacity and a few good people who could look beyond the stereotype. And ironically, the more heavily tattooed I have become, the more I have been stereotyped.

As a woman with a disability, a woman with a guide dog and heavily tattooed, I have the odds stacked against me the moment I walk into a new place. To feel welcomed is an unusual sensation for me. This is what makes it all the more precious when I do find places and people who are non-judgmental and do not actually judge a book by its cover.

New Life Partners

"I'm going on a blind date tomorrow in Brisbane." We were celebrating being happily single at an anti-Valentine's party that has become a bit of a traditional gathering amongst my friends.

Excitement was bubbling inside me, making my stomach do little flips. Bob, my good friend, drove me to Brisbane, and from there, I took the train to where I was to meet my date. Would we get on? Would he like me? How would he react when he first met me? Over and over in my mind, the questions played. I desperately wanted us to be compatible.

When we finally came face to face at the pre-arranged meeting spot, he was beautifully mannered, even allowing me to reach out and touch him. He did not flinch as I moved closer. We took to each other immediately, and I could not wait to update my status on Facebook. I wanted to shout my news from the rooftops.

"In a relationship with Keegan."

"Wow! 2 hours from meeting! You're a fast worker, girl!" was my friend, Chrisy's response.

In Gaelic baby names, the meaning of the name Keegan is small and fiery. In Irish baby names, the meaning of the name Keegan is a thinker; fiery. And here is me, a fiery Irish redhead that has fought for my own rights for more years than I can remember. The fact that we were a perfect pair made me ask myself whether this was actually a fluke or was it divine intervention, a special gift from Lugh, the Celtic God of Justice and Mischief?

Keegan's arrival signified a new chapter in my life. I am not Keegan's owner and never will be. He is owned by Guide Dogs Queensland, and everyone who is allocated a dog is officially known as a handler.

On 24 March, Keegan and I moved in together. We were allocated Room 2, at the in-house live in training centre for Guide Dogs Queensland in Bald Hills. This was to be our home for the next seven days where we were to undergo training for our new life together. Our seven days together were interrupted on Monday 29th March.

"Janice, you need to go to your room, grab your stuff and we'll get you home."

The three of us in training handlers and our dogs were being sent home early because South East Queensland was entering another lock down.

It is a Guide Dog requirement that new handlers and dogs spend the first two weeks building their unique bond of trust and understanding. In our case, this was made easier by the fact that the entire South East Queensland community was in lock down. Keegan is an unusual dog, extremely affectionate and highly intuitive as well as intelligent. We have created a powerful bond and even though I am called 'his handler', our relationship is seriously special.

I was at the psychologist recently; he started asking questions about the way that I had been discriminated against, affecting me. I became upset talking about it. Keegan, who had been lying under my chair, stood up and started to comfort me. He put one paw on my left shoulder, and one paw on my right shoulder and hugged me. Keegan is 100% worth the three years I had to wait to be allocated a dog.

Adventures of Keegan the Guide Dog is a Facebook page I created to help create community awareness of life as and with a guide dog; it has allowed me to share insights into life for and with Keegan.

Out of the blue, a beautiful surprise came in the form of a private Facebook message that arrived from a lady called Helen Lipscombe. I discovered, through her message, the pivotal role she had played in the foundation months of Keegan's life.

"Hi Keegan, this is a message for your mummy Janice.

I was so happy today to be told about Keegan's page. I am his first raiser, from 8 weeks, so did all the home and socialising skills. He was the most lovable puppy. I am so happy that he is happy and working for you and with you.

It is really tough to give up these puppies, but it is really worth it when I see what they do to enhance a life like yours. Great to see you allow him up on the furniture. Guide Dogs don't allow the puppies on furniture just in case the client won't let them.

I love that you have such an active and varied life. Keegan was Guide Dog #2 for us, I have been invited to his graduation and I would also love to forward you his wee puppy photo's. He was so cute. Thank you for loving him, as I can see that you do."

Hearing from Helen, receiving the puppy photos and having her attend Keegan's graduation deeply touched me. I was so used to being totally alone, and now, connecting with people who had showered limitless love on a puppy that they were never going to be able to keep was surreal for me.

When Helen offered to make a mortarboard for Keegan to wear at his graduation. I happily accepted; Helen added a green tassel trim in acknowledgement of my Irish heritage, which matched the green tie I chose for him to wear for the occasion. The Guide Dogs used this photograph of Keegan taken to mark the occasion as part of their publicity.

Keegan does love to be dressed up, and it gives me great joy to choose outfits for him to wear at some of the fun festivals and events we attend together. Playful and loving, Keegan likes nothing better than to run free, roll around in the grass, and bask in the sun, yet the moment his harness comes out, he transforms into a dutiful, fully alert working Guide Dog.

Through Facebook, I also heard from Rosemary Walker. "Not many raisers get to see the journey their beloved pup heads towards. They don't see them grow and mature and live their lives helping and being important. Nor do they see the love that grows – that wonderful bond that just shines out of you and your boy. So special – brings tears of joy to a lot of wonderful people who got him to you." Rosemary is a puppy raiser who knew Keegan's mother and was also her raiser.

I love being connected to those who brought Keegan into my life and am eternally grateful he had such a wonderful start to his life. Having no family of my own, thanks to my abusive upbringing and my disastrous marriage, I find enormous fulfilment and comfort in loving Keegan.

"You'll be sorry to see him go," are the words that regularly greet me when I am out with Keegan in a shopping centre. Being commonly mistaken for a guide dog trainer is pretty much normal for me, even though Keegan is in his harness emblazoned with the words Guide Dog.

There is nothing wrong with my actual eyes. My eyes look perfectly normal. They are clear and bright without any scarring, clouding or cataracts. The kind of vision impairment I live with was caused by the damage I sustained to my brain during the surgery to supposedly help my epilepsy.

"Your camera is nearly perfect, but you don't have a computer to plug it into," was how the eye surgeon I went to visit in September 2019 explained my situation. "Neurosurgery will have to be performed before I can do any eye surgery."

My answer to the neurosurgeon was, "I'll have a chat to myself over a few drinks about this."

The chat with myself was short. There was no way I was going to let anyone operate on my head again. As much as I would enjoy having my vision,

I am doing okay even if I am becoming more visually impaired with each passing year.

In some cases, people with my condition find that glasses may help to improve double vision through the use of prisms. Immediately after the operation, I had tunnel vision. I could see clearly what was directly in front of me and after a while, I became used to only seeing straight ahead and this became my new normal. Today, I have a tiny pinprick of vision in daylight and rely heavily on colour. I see blurred shapes without any detail, and once the sun goes down and darkness falls, I am living in a world of total blindness.

I do have a range of glasses. One for reading my laptop screen, which is my lifeline to the outside world, another set to read my phone and specific glasses to see my food. When it comes to food, it is impossible for me to distinguish chicken, from mashed potato or cauliflower because they all look alike. It is the same blur of colour to me on a plate. Similarly, carrots, sweet potatoes and pumpkin all blend together because they are one colour.

More correctly, the glasses I have are powerful magnifiers, and they do not correct my vision in the way a pair of prescribed glasses from the optometrist does. Things are a blur with or without my glasses.

I always tell my friends never to ask me, "How do I look?" or "Does this lipstick look good on me?" because I am never able to see the details. I can see faces, but never any depth. I do not know if someone has wrinkles or blemishes, a big nose, or is pretty or downright ugly.

One of the advantages of not being able to see clearly is that I have never judged anyone on their appearance. I guess this is why I have been so disappointed every time that I am judged based only on my appearance.

I, quite literally, have not got the brains left inside my head for my eyes to function. I am neurologically blind. There are no scars or physical deformities that are visible, which makes it difficult for people to understand that I am blind. I look like I can see, I know there is a face, and I can turn to look directly at your face or where the voice is coming from; this gives the appearance that I am able to see, which confuses the heck out of people.

Travelling around the world as a single woman alone, it was safer not to let anyone know I was blind. It is thanks to the perfectly normal look of my eyes that I managed to travel without anyone knowing that I was blind. On the plus side, this means I can donate my eyes to medical science when I do eventually depart this world.

They say having a guide dog allows you freedom and independence. You can supposedly go anywhere you want and do whatever you want, if it is legal, without limitations. Unfortunately, thanks to today's discriminatory society, I often get refused entry into hotels, pubs, cafes, restaurants, accommodation, transport, and pretty much everywhere I go.

Being refused access is in breach of federal legislation and there are hefty fines in place when an establishment is reported.

As a guide dog handler, I am issued an identification document that I need to have with me and be able to produce when asked. Keegan needs to be wearing his official Guide Dog harness. If he is not wearing his harness, he is off duty, and there are no special concessions for him. The harness is his uniform.

When refused entry, it is my habit to ask to speak to the manager. I like to try and amicably explain that they are making an error, but this does not always work. It is hard to believe that despite guide dogs having been in Australia for over 50 years and the legislation that is in place, we are still experiencing discrimination on a regular basis. There is a 99% chance I will be refused entry because of Keegan. In rare instances, it is a genuine lack of awareness.

The level of discrimination against our wonderful animal helpers who bring their handlers so much freedom has been a real eye-opener (pardon the pun). I make a point of always letting the establishment know that I do plan to report their actions; I suspect that some of them have thought that I was just sounding off with an empty threat. I do not like confrontations, and yet when it comes to injustice or discrimination, I have never hesitated to report breaches. My hackles rise, and I feel duty bound to try to ensure others have an easier time gaining access; I know not everyone has the same courage, but neither did I to start off with.

Speaking up for myself is something I have gradually learnt to do. Today, no matter how big the organization or the fact that they are a giant household name will stop me from following up for justice.

What I am seeking each time I take action is for staff education to take place, for policies to be improved and for an apology for myself. Trying to browbeat me by standing firm and refusing to admit there is an issue never works with me. I will go toe to toe and stand up for my rights. I have won all my cases, and, in most instances, these victories have resulted in changes to company policies. Where possible, I do make a point of going back to the establishments with Keegan to see that the promised changes have happened; sometimes, it is smooth sailing and at other times, the establishments allow us in reluctantly.

In Emerald, I was refused entry into two Chinese restaurants on one night because of Keegan. I did not eat that night and went to bed hungry. The next morning, I was straight on the phone to the advocacy group, Blind Citizens Australia. Martin, the advocate, rang both establishments and went to great lengths to explain that their actions were illegal. I received an apology. More important than the apology is that awareness has been created. Both these restaurants are now fully aware that hefty fines can be imposed next time they discriminate against someone with an assistance dog.

On the flip side of this coin are the venues that are part of national franchise chains. Some even have a sign up that reads, "Guide Dogs Welcome", and yet we were refused entry.

It is a sad situation to say that it is easier to stay home where I am not going to be discriminated against. My feisty Irish fighting spirit comes to the fore when I am faced with discrimination.

I fight not only for myself but for all those other people who are struggling with their disabilities and may not have the same willpower or ability to speak up to make their voices heard.

A part of me is shy and afraid, yet when I am in public and there are people around me, I feel safe.

Once I managed to gain my freedom, once I became confident to speak up, my voice is something I have never allowed to be stifled.

Using my voice to create improvements in the world and correct what I see to be injustices gives me enormous satisfaction, even if I am quaking on the inside. After all, if no one speaks up, then the situation will never improve. I might only be one voice, but small actions do eventually add up, and changes begin to happen. Eventually.

Blind Citizens Australia are the national representative body that supports people like me who are blind or vision impaired. They have been the most wonderful source of information on my rights, helping me to advocate and help resolve situations that have involved national franchise coffee chains and restaurants discriminating against myself and Keegan.

The Royal Blind Society, which is now known as Vision Australia, first recommended Blind Citizens Australia to me when I was attending TAFE studying retail. Thoroughly enjoying the course, I was surprised to be told when it came to the visual merchandise subject that because I was visually impaired, it would not be possible for me to do visual merchandise. Enraged at being forced out of the class and then, to add insult to injury, being told that I was not going to be allowed to finish the course, I rang Blind Citizens Australia.

The advocate, Aileen, after listening to my story, asked what I expected as an outcome. I wanted an apology from every teacher that was involved in it, including the head honcho of the course. My needs were simple, I wanted to be allowed to complete the course. Most importantly, I wanted changes to policies and procedures at the TAFE.

Aileen arranged for mediation. I won. But and there is always a but, with the condition that instead of me going to the TAFE to actively participate in the visual marketing class, they would send a teacher to my craft shop.

I must be fair and confess that having the tutor in my workspace did give me bonus benefits. I got to implement in my workspace exactly what was being taught. It was discriminatory and absolutely ridiculous, but thanks to Blind Citizens Australia, I got my Certificate IV in Retail.

Running

I have, for the majority of my adult life, always said, "running is against my religion". I could not think of anything worse than going for a run. The thought of that kind of activity being remotely fun was a thought that never crossed my mind. The only kind of running I was ever into was running away. I have become accomplished at running for my life.

When I moved to Queensland, I knew hardly anyone. In one of the sessions with my psychologist, I shared that I was experiencing feelings of extreme isolation. He mentioned the word 'parkrun'. The words run and exercise were an anathema to me.

Inwardly squirming, but sitting still because I have manners, I listened politely as he shared his reasoning for recommending parkrun. The benefits were that this global movement, the brainchild of Paul Sinton-Hewitt, (who decided that the spelling should be with a lower-case p and all one word) was a positive, welcoming and inclusive experience. There was no time limit, and no one finished last.

Speaking from his own personal experience as a participant, he persuasively explained that the runs were held every Saturday morning and 100% free. It would cost me nothing to go, so what did I have to lose? His reasoning made sense, and to make it even harder for me to refuse; there was a parkrun down the road from where I was living.

Reassuringly I learnt that I did not have to run the 5 kilometres. Plenty of people walked, pushed prams, and took their dogs, kids and grandkids. No one would make fun of me.

As my psychologist waited expectantly for me to respond, I figured there was no way I could wiggle out of at least giving it a try. At least that way, I could say I had done as he suggested, and it was most certainly not for me.

On Saturday 30th of March 2019, I turned up at the North Lakes parkrun accompanied by my friend Bob who had agreed to act as my guide. Not expecting to enjoy the experience, I was surprised at the feeling of acceptance and welcome that enveloped me.

I turned up again the next week and the one after that. Without consciously realising what was happening, it became my Saturday morning habit. A parkrun often followed by the social interaction of coffee and a chat. Surprisingly, I was actually enjoying myself and looked forward to these outings.

During my sixth session, as I was walking with Bob, I decided that I wanted to run rather than walk. As Bob tried to dissuade me from the idea, I let go of the tether and started to run, leaving Bob behind. I must have looked like a weirdo with my arms and legs going in all directions as I tried to run. When Bob caught up with me, common sense kicked in; I was lucky not to have injured myself running off on my own without a guide.

The idea of running rather than walking offered me a new challenge that I made my mind up to tackle. Following a bit of research, I discovered there were experienced running guides that would help me. I put a post on Facebook and ended up with Tracey, from Achilles Brisbane, which is part of the global Achilles International network. She was amazing.

The guides certainly live up to their mission statement, "Achilles International transforms the lives of people with disabilities through athletic programs and social connection." I was hooked on running and used Achilles for months attempting to beat my personal best every week.

I would sometimes use visual aids instead of a support runner. The visual aids make the parkrun safe by telling me if a bike is passing, whether there are overhanging branches, if I need to go uphill or downhill, where there are uneven surfaces, and change of directions etc. It is all done by voice.

The more I ran, the more hooked I became. I felt a sense of freedom and an adrenaline rush each time I set off on a parkrun.

When I discovered the parkrun app and found out about the additional challenges available as part of parkrun, and there are many, it became my mission to complete them. At times I regret that I did not know about parkrun when I was on my international globetrotting travels. There are some cool runs that I would love to be able to complete.

Being philosophical, and in retrospect, it was not the right time in my life for me to have considered taking up running for pleasure. At that stage, as I moved from country to country, I was doing a different kind of running; I was running for my life.

Now, I am in a position where I am relaxed enough to be able to run for personal enjoyment, exercise and my mental health as opposed to running for my life. By way of introduction, I will often say, 'my body is as colourful as my personality.'

Wanting others on the parkrun to understand I was blind without having to have an awkward conversation I had a pink singlet printed with the words BLIND RUNNER. It has since become a bit of a trademark for me to turn up wearing fun T-shirts or singlets to each of the parkruns.

In February 2021, I got a little braver and ordered another custom singlet emblazoned with the words BLIND BY DAY, DRUNK BY NIGHT along with one that reads WILL RUN FOR WINE; these three running tops that I rotate through always get comments and are great icebreakers when I turn up at new places each week.

Never in a million years did I think I would give up drinking with friends on a Friday night so I could get up at 3 am or 5 am to go for a 5k run on Saturday morning. But the beautiful fresh air, friendly community and health benefits keep me returning every week.

My first challenge, which fittingly began with A, was the Alphabet Challenge. As the name suggests, the aim is to complete a parkrun in locations that correspond with the letters of the alphabet. There is one letter missing and that is the letter X. Interestingly, with all the exotic locations all over the globe, there is no location anywhere in the world starting with that letter that has a parkrun.

Many individuals who have been doing parkrun for years choose to go to the same runs each week. As a travel junkie, I love traversing the country to the different runs. Most of my runs were completed in Queensland, apart from two of the letters of the alphabet.

I headed to Wheelers Hill in Victoria to do the Jells parkrun, and to Casino, in New South Wales to tick off the letter Q with the Queen Elizabeth parkrun. Getting the alphabet ticked off took me 2 years; it would have been a lot quicker had COVID-19, and the New South Wales and Queensland floods not set me back about nine months.

When parkruns resumed in November 2020, I could not wait for Saturday morning to roll around. Being immuno-compromised crowds needed to be avoided for the sake of my physical health. Carefully considering my options, I made the deliberately measured decision to only attend the smaller runs with less than 50 participants. My first run was at Oakey, Toowoomba, with 41 participants.

The Staying Alive Challenge was a perfect one for me to cross off my list since I've spent the last 25+ years staying alive myself despite the odds being stacked against me. This challenge has an interesting history and a sense of humour. Participants must complete 3 B and 3 G parkruns. A little fun fact I discovered is that when the Gibb brothers moved to Australia in 1958, they began playing on the radio with friends Bill Goode and Bill Gates. The group's name was originally The BG's from the common initials between Barry Gibb, Bill Goode, and Bill Gates. The name then evolved from The BG's to the Bee Gees, which eventually came to mean the Brothers Gibb.

Keegan came into my life in March 2021. The first run we did together was Toowoomba on 3rd April 2021. Keegan loves the runs; he enjoys his Saturday morning trips to whatever parkrun is on the schedule and enjoys his treat afterwards for doing a great job.

I no longer need to use Achilles or any guides. As we travel to complete our parkruns, I believe we are also spreading awareness about approaching a working guide dog as well as the rights of people with disabilities.

Keegan is great as he automatically makes the change of direction, avoids uneven surfaces, guides me around other runners, avoids overhanging branches etc. We run to our own rhythm, and most other runners respect our space.

"Any first timers?" parkrun organisers no matter where you go, always ask the question. My hand shoots up every weekend because I am always a first timer as I choose to do a different run each week.

Being a first timer means the organizer takes you aside to provide a briefing and description of the run. About three words into the description, I am lost. My acquired brain injury prevents me from being able to understand the instructions being given. Thankfully, having Keegan running with me means I will never be lost; it also means that unless I am the only entrant, I will never be first! But I could not care less about being first as long as I get to participate.

Keegan knows to follow the scent on the track left by the other runners ahead of us. The scent tells him the way to lead me, even when we have never been to that place before. He is exceptional at his job.

The kids on the runs love to come up to Keegan, which is flattering, but as he is a working guide dog, I spend time each week explaining what his harness means.

Interacting and teaching the children about guide dogs is truly enjoyable as their young sponge-like brains are super receptive, and they are always keen to listen. Keegan's harness comes off once we have finished our run allowing the kids to pat and make a fuss over him; he absolutely loves all the attention and willingly poses for photographs.

Volunteering and giving back to an event that has opened up a whole new world for me is something I feel strongly driven to contribute to. After running on Saturday, I usually volunteer on Sunday to assist with the junior parkrun.

The sense of camaraderie and community amongst participants is infectious as the early morning air fills with welcome greetings to newcomers and regular participants alike. I love that there are no winners and that we are there to participate and challenge ourselves. A bonus is the fact that there is no time limit. When I started parkrun being able to go at my own pace with no pressure was a massive attraction for me; there is even a tail walker making sure no one gets lost or left behind on the runs; I've volunteered in this role 41 times so far. In the beginning, I used to always be bringing up the rear, but as time has gone past, my stamina and speed gradually improved. Improving on my personal best each time is my goal.

The Airlie Beach run was the finish of my Cowell Club challenge. This challenge is named after Chris and Linda Cowell, the first male and female runners who participated at 100 different parkrun events. For someone who was 'allergic to running' I totally surprised myself when I realised, I was about to tick off my 100th run.

My memory may not be the best, but the parkrun app on my phone is a wonderful tool for me to track and maintain a record of what I have completed and what I want to tackle. It has all the events I participated in and helps me recall where I have been and on what dates.

My 100th run was worth a celebration. I treated myself to a luxury stay on Hamilton Island in an underwater suite for Keegan and myself. True, I could not properly see all the marine life on the other side of our glass windows, but I wanted to be able to go through the experience.

The landmark run is embedded firmly in my memory banks as a truly special occasion because the volunteers and participants at Airlie Beach parkrun were extremely welcoming. It sounds like a cliché to use the word fantastic, but that is exactly what it was. As Keegan was leading me towards the finish line, I could make out the blurry outlines of bodies standing in what seemed like a row on either side of the finish flag. I think there were about 12 of them, but with my vision impairment, it was impossible to be sure. I heard their cheers ringing out, and as we got closer, their voices and clapping echoed in my ears. As we crossed the line, I realised that, unbelievably they had formed a guard of honour, for me!

"Oh my God, this is embarrassing," flashed through my mind. Simultaneously I felt a frisson of pride, achievement, amazement, and pleasure course through my body as I stumbled across the finish line. I had done it!

Airlie Beach was the friendliest parkrun that I have ever been to. The welcome and warmth from the runners went a long way to making up for the appalling discrimination Keegan, and I had faced elsewhere during our stay. Considering Airlie Beach is a tourism destination and a gateway to the Great Barrier Reef, I was taken aback and completely surprised to find the level of discrimination that existed against a woman with a Guide Dog.

When I am asked what makes me addicted to parkrun, I can truthfully say, "I think the reason I'm so into parkrun is because of the warm welcome and the crazy challenges. When you come to think of it, my entire life has been one continuous challenge".

My Next Challenge

In early 2021, I was starting to have serious trouble with my memory. I have always had memory issues, but this time it was different. It was frightening and a totally new situation to find myself in.

I would be sitting at home when the next thing I was conscious of was being in a totally different place with absolutely no recollection of how I got there. Places like out on the road or close to the railway tracks. These experiences occurred more regularly and were nothing like my epilepsy seizures. Feeling sufficiently scared, I forced myself to overcome my fear of the medical professional.

I sought out a female doctor and made an appointment. My first thought was that I had Alzheimer's. Following tests conducted in the surgery I was reassured I did not have Alzheimer's.

"But considering you've had brain surgery, we're going to send you in for a scan," she handed over the referral form.

I spent the weekend anxiously counting down the hours to my Monday visit to the doctor. I would be receiving the results of the scan done on Friday.

The report from the scan was written in medical language, words I had never heard of.

"Can you please speak English?" I requested.

The scan showed that my brain was being eaten away. The cause stems back to the removal of my left temporal lobe; it means the nerves on the right side of the brain are growing and spreading across the left. They are trying to compensate for what was removed. But instead of healthy cells growing, these cells are causing my body to deteriorate.

My brain is shrinking, being eaten away; I have been legally blind for the bulk of my life and as I age, my sight is deteriorating more rapidly. At the time of writing this, I see things in quadruple, and it is hard to focus on anything; there is a considerable amount of blurring, and I am no longer able to see colour.

I have an acquired brain injury and am a lifelong epileptic; there are plenty of times in my life when I could easily have given up. But then, something deep inside me stirs to life. Fight harder, scream louder.

You are the only person who has control over your life; today could be your last day so enjoy every minute of it.

When I was told that I was too dumb to study, I went and studied to prove the assessor wrong. After being told that I would never be able to walk again, here I am, walking and even running.

My husband used to threaten me if I ever left, "You will be single for the rest of your fucking life." He was right.

I will be single for the rest of my life BUT that is my choice. I am happy being single. I can choose my own clothes, wear a bikini, bright eye popping colours, tight jeans, or shorts.

I also have the freedom to go out when I want, eat what I want, talk to anyone and everyone, travel anywhere, voice my opinions and even hold the remote control. I will never allow myself to be abused or controlled by a partner again.

It is hard for outsiders to understand why I choose to live on my own, especially since I cannot drive and need support for my shopping, cleaning, and everyday tasks that fully sighted people take for granted.

I was 100% controlled for so long; being diagnosed with Battered Wife Syndrome means being able to live my life without anyone questioning what I am doing or why is crucial to my ongoing mental wellbeing.

Today, thanks to the funding I receive from the NDIS, I can choose my own support services. I have a spreadsheet to track the funding that is allocated and where and how it is spent. Keeping close track of the services I am using; I decide whom I want to help me with my accessibility and goals.

Finding honest and ethical support can be a challenge as unscrupulous service providers and support workers see recipients of the NDIS as cash cows.

As the NDIS began the trial in Newcastle, I was one of the first recipients to receive a small amount of funding. The funds were specifically to help meet the cost of a cleaner. It was minimal funding, but I was grateful to be a recipient.

When I opened the door to let in my new cleaner, the woman standing on the doorstep burst into a fit of laughter. She was laughing so hard that she could not talk.

Indicating for her to follow me, we climbed the stairs to my studio, where Jodie introduced herself and apologized for her inappropriate laughter, explaining that the agency had told her I was tattooed but, despite their warning, she had not expected the gloriously coloured canvas that opened the door to her. At least she was honest. It turned out she was a useless cleaner but had a fun personality. We hit it off and Jodie transitioned from being my cleaner to being the person who took me out and about when I needed support. We became and remain friends to this day.

Thriving, healing, and living life to the full despite the circumstances that we each face are the legacy I want to leave. The power lies inside each one of us to choose whether we accept our fate or we decide to fight for what is our right. The right to live in a secure, safe and free environment where we are unafraid to express ourselves.

Today, I have a roof over my head. My own home. It is a far cry from those days of sleeping under the bridge in Sydney. I have the fantastic company of Keegan, my Guide Dog and one of the biggest things of all is that living on my own, I have full control of the remote for the TV. Seriously, that is a big deal to me. If I decide to go out for a walk, I can go. If I want to eat chocolate, I can. No one is going to question or punish me.

There are some things I cannot do that are related to my epilepsy, but the restrictions are mostly diet related. Hot chocolate, topped with marshmallows, is my drink of choice, as I cannot have coffee under any circumstances. Luckily, I can enjoy alcohol without triggering a seizure. The keto diet I follow does mean using talking scales to help ensure I measure correctly, as this is an essential part of keeping my seizures under control without prescription medications. What works for me may not work for other epileptics, as each of us is unique and individual.

The memory of being constantly wrapped in a thick fog caused by my medication means it is easy for me to remain disciplined and stick to a strict diet. I never want to go back to that place of numbness and will do everything in my power to keep the fog from swirling around to envelop me again.

The lesson I have learnt on this journey through life is that the world is in my hands. There is no point in choosing to blame others. The past is behind me, and the only thing I can control is how I react to situations.

Having struggled through significant life challenges, I recall feeling lost at sea without a life raft or support crew in sight. My brain, my physical body and my memory have all been affected. It has been a struggle to piece together the fragments of my memories. At times, it has been like doing a jigsaw puzzle and looking for the missing pieces to work out which bit goes where and how everything fits together.

If I offend people, if they are put off by the language I may sometimes use, or the colourful canvas that is my appearance, that is because they are viewing my actions and behaviour through their own prism. That prism is shaped and influenced by their childhood, by the experiences they went through and the people they encountered along their journey.

We each have the opportunity to choose whether to learn from our experiences, to rise above them or to wallow in self-pity at our unfortunate circumstances. How we choose to react is the one thing within our control. We cannot control the circumstances or reactions of others; only our own.

I have made a choice to live my life with gratitude. Yes, gratitude. Despite everything that life has thrown at me, I have ultimately come to understand that we each have, inside of us, what we need to recover. Sometimes we need professional help to unpack and understand the power that we hold.

It is up to us to control the narrative of our lives. It is easy to sit back and feel sorry for yourself, to accept the role of victim. I am a survivor, not a victim.

Choosing to reframe the circumstances of my birth, the epilepsy that I was born with, and the medical verdict that I would not live beyond 25 has allowed me to experience life to the fullest. It has certainly not been an easy process, but this is the process that has made me the person I am today.

I have come to learn that there is no timeline to this process of recovery. It cannot be hurried, and many people give up; I admit I have at times. When you repeatedly hear, "just give up, you're never gonna get there, you're never gonna get anywhere," it is easy to give in.

For me, that is when my "Fuck You" attitude comes to the fore I'm the fiery Irish lassie who has finally found herself and discovered her voice. When they told me I would not live beyond 25, I challenged that prognosis every step of the way. Despite the challenges of learning to walk again, of running for my life and of having to make a completely fresh start, I was grateful.

Grateful for each year that I have been granted, grateful for being able to summon the courage to finally leave my husband, and grateful for the opportunities that opened up for me when all seemed dark and lost.

Whether you have or are currently experiencing domestic violence, disability, sexual abuse, discrimination, homelessness, or failure of the system, the power lies within you to change your circumstances. It is the inward focus on yourself that will give you the clarity to make the decision on which path to take and more importantly, when to take it.

When you realise and accept that you hold the power, rather than the perpetrator, the offender or the system, you find the strength to start to move forward. It is your journey, and it is your decision to choose which path to take and most importantly when to take that path. As I write these words, it sounds simple. The reality is that simple and easy are two completely different things.

Well intentioned people who have not travelled your road tell you to build a bridge and get over what you have been through. It is not that easy. When you have had surgery and you lose your sight, you cannot just build a bridge and get over it because it is there forever. You are scarred forever. I cannot just forget about it. Instead, you have to learn a completely new way of living. To this day, I have an absolute fear of being in a room alone with a male; even if the doors are open, I cannot do it.

It takes considerable energy and a lot out of you. You must work your way along a long, long uneven trail for getting around the bridge rather than over it. Sometimes, they make it out as if someone is going to give you a pair of wings so you can just fly over that bridge, and everything will go away. Each of us has a different experience. And mine has been that this is a hard, rough trial. You think you can go one way, but it leads to a massive drop off a cliff.

You must turn around, go back; not the whole way back but enough to try another trail with a knife in hand to chop your way through the bushes to carve your own corridor. And then you come to something else blocking the way; once again, you go back that little bit more to find another way through.

This is what I have been doing all my life, working to find my way around the bridge. And even today, I am continuing to find my way around that bridge. I cannot simply walk over it.

I guess I have learned how to manipulate myself in the sense that when I come to that cliff, I do not just give up and jump off. I make that corridor; I forge my own path no matter what obstacles come up along the route.

"You've had a shit life, Janice" is how some friends describe my circumstances.

Yes, it has been shitty for most of the first 40 years, and yet, I now have Keegan, the love of my life; we live in a comfortable home that is my own. I travel as the whim takes me and have a small but true circle of friends.

Regardless of how imperfect my life has been, once I understood that I had the ability to control my reactions, I have always chosen to turn my face towards the sun and live life to the full.

After losing my vision, I backpacked around the world alone, and my inner eyes were opened despite my lack of sight. I starred in movies, documentaries, magazines, books, and television series.

My experiences have included meeting and working with many famous celebrities on my journey, and they are no different to anyone else.

Every single person is a unique human being, each of us has personal fears to conquer and mountains to climb, except in some cases the mountains are higher and the path to the summit much steeper.

Although my life has been difficult and rocky since the day I arrived in the world on St Patrick's Day, 17th March, I have somehow always managed to find a way to see the positive side of life. I truly believe in always looking for the positive side of life regardless of the situation and surroundings.

I am lucky to be alive. The wounds that have been inflicted on me are now no longer festering scabs. Whilst I have struggled with the lack of public acceptance of my appearance and disability, I have now totally accepted myself, my past and even my future.

Speaking of the future, no one knows how long we have left in the world, and each day needs to be lived to the fullest. My plans are to continue running. I am no longer running from the offender or abuser but running because it brings me happiness and fulfilment; every Saturday morning at parkrun and volunteering at the children's runs every Sunday morning with Keegan brings me immeasurable joy. I have come full circle from running from domestic violence, running for my life, to running blind because I love it.

The doctors who said I would not live beyond 25 were wrong. The assessor who said I was too dumb was wrong.

How long will I live? No one knows.

"Only the good die young," is what my friend, Barbra, reminds me. "And because you're a bitch, you're gonna live forever."

My answer to that is, "It's Miss Bitch to you."

A small selection of poems I have been drawn to write about specific events and periods of my life.

They have never been shared publicly.

I WAS TOLD!!!

I'd be dead by the age of 25,
But now I'm 50 and still alive.
I will never be able to walk again,
But I can wobble to the drinker's den.
Never would I be able to hold a conversation,
But I can, thanks to pure dedication.
I'd never be able to board a plane,
But I've travelled the world in pure vain.
I will never regain my sense of touch,
So, I gave up on contact pretty much
I would forever be dependent on someone,
But now I independently attend the parkrun.
Never would I have a sense of taste,
So yeah, food without texture is just a waste.
I will never have a sense of smell,
So, it has affected my eating as well.
I will live the rest of my life blind,
But I can hear music, so I don't mind.

EPILEPSY IS DANCING

I get a strange taste in my mouth,
Knowing my body will soon go south.
Yep, I'm having another aura,
Which tells me a seizure is just around the corner.
I fight this terror in my mind,
My vision of you is all too kind.
It can last a few minutes or up to an hour,
I have no control nor any power.
My body stiffens and becomes so strong,
My limbs start dancing, it looks so wrong.
Epilepsy is dancing, it's dancing with me,
Please, just one song and let it be.
My seizure will eventually complete,
My body now feels defeat.
I'm tired, I'm exhausted, I need to sleep,
I lay my body and soul to keep.

disABILITY

I can drive a computer but not a car,
But luckily the pub isn't too far.

I can ride a partner but not a bike,
It's only my eyes that went on strike.

I can fly around the world but not a kite,
It's a bit hard to see it when I have no sight.

I can sail the seven seas but not a yacht,
I am blind, in case you forgot.

I can do a Parkrun but not a marathon,
Tomorrow's Saturday, so bring it on!

#FUCK COVID19

Whilst doctors and nurses put their life on the line,
I isolate at home and drink a bottle of wine.
The police are in force handing out social distancing fines,
Whilst I've just drank another twelve wines.
The government hands out funds for people to survive,
Whilst us forgotten one's struggle to stay alive.
Support workers show their greed,
Rather than help the people in need.
Hoping this pandemic will come to an end,
Then the entire world can be on the mend.
In the meantime, here I am at home alone,
Waiting and waiting and waiting for the unknown...

I SURRENDER

They say no, but I say yes,

Argh! who cares, I'm already a mess.

So today, sweet and innocent me,

Surrenders her body, to him, JC.

My will is totally up to date,

And I've signed my papers 'Do Not Resuscitate'

My head will hurt, and my heart will pound,

I'll have no vision but plenty of sound.

Yep, today's the day I take the test,

If all goes well and I do pass,

Or if I do lose to fate,

Don't bother with the pearly gate,

Just say goodbye to this stupid clod,

And return me to She, our Irish God...

MY INNER CHILD

I'm not for hire, I'm not for sale,
Still today I stay clear of male.

You knowingly put me in this situation,
Just to please your infatuation.

I rise high, as high as can be,
Escaping from you, I became free.

THE UNKNOWN

I lie awake with so many things on my mind,
I just want to run and leave everything behind.
I have nobody. No family or friends,
I want off this ride. Here's where it ends.
I don't like aggression, I'm too scared to speak,
The potential results are not what I seek.
The fear is real, so very real,
It's time to leave and start to heal.

THE RECOVERY

Emotional abuse leaves even bigger scars,
Than the physical abuse that makes you see stars.
The abuser has no self-esteem,
Therefore, wants to feel supreme.
So, if your partner doesn't treat you right,
Just leave on the first possible flight.
You are beautiful inside and out,
I know that without a doubt.

LOVE SHOULDN'T HURT

YOU SAY...
Do as I say, not as I do,
Don't even think about it or I'll flatten you.
You are weak and I am strong,
You have known this all along.
Where's dinner? I've had a shit day, can't you see,
You wouldn't be here if it wasn't for me!
Go on a diet, you're getting too fat,
I might respect you after that.

I SAY...
I lay in this bed by your side,
Thinking where I could possibly hide,
I want to run, I want to be free,
Because I hate the way you treat me.
Every day is all about you,
I'm here, do I even exist too!
I've put on some weight but I'm still ok,
You don't have to talk to me that way.

NEVER SAY 'NEVER'

Yeah, I'm fucked. I'm legally blind,
But I've lost my sight, not my mind.
My kids call me 'The Blind Bat',
Plus other things along with that!
I have very limited tunnel vision,
And the Celtic Gods put me on this mission.
I see very little in daylight,
But have no vision at all when it comes to night.
In light I see double and blur, it's hard to explain,
And at night I rely on you or my cane.
Yet I fulfill my life every single day,
I won't allow my blindness to get in the way.
I'm like a bird, as free as can be,
I enjoy life just being me.
I'm a free spirit, what can I say,
I travel the world day by day.
Yeah, life can sometimes get pretty hard.
But I just move on and pick the next card.
Just be yourself and enjoy your day,
If you need an ear, I'm just a phone call away.
Never say 'never',
Not now, not ever!

TILL DEATH DO US PART

The relationship was a very violent storm,
My beatings and imprisonment were just the norm.
I was waiting for that fatal day,
When a crazy woman came my way.
Dragging me from one police station to another,
We found a detective, who became my big brother.
He took my hand and got down on his knee,
And there he was proposing to me.
The proposal was music filled with delight,
It was then my decision to fight or flight.
I fled the country and went straight home,
There I was diagnosed with battered wife syndrome.
I had to change my name and appearance,
To cross another border and be given a clearance.
I travelled the world so far and wide,
Being on the run with nowhere to hide.
Few scars are visible from the torture endured,
But the pain inside will never be cured.
There became a day when I could no longer run,

RUNNING FOR MY LIFE

I just wanted to be with my number one.
I walk on eggshells in fear every day,
That monster could anytime come my way.
After being granted a nice bodyguard,
My new life became a picture postcard.
I now feel free, safe and secure,
My life became better, that's for sure.
Along this journey, I met you,
We became close friends out of the blue.
You always fill my life with fun and laughter,
And I hope to return the favour forever after.
You are now tattooed across my heart,
And I truly hope we never part.

'THE' TATTOO

I'm the tattoo that people ask about,
What's the story behind it? They all shout.

I seem to stand out above the rest,
That I put many minds to the test.

I see what she cannot see,
And without her knowledge, she touches me.

Am I on her right or on her left,
Do I represent her abuse or maybe a death.

Or maybe I'm somewhere in the middle,
A combination of both could be the riddle.

I am here and I'm here to stay,
Her memories of me will never fade away.

Yes, I have now become a public tattoo,
But she got me for herself, not for you.

So don't ask questions and don't ask why,
Because as always, she will start to cry.

So if you see me, you can look, but please don't stare,
Show her some respect with tender loving care.

You may be curious but please never ask,
As she'll have to ease the pain with a 5 litre cask.
In her album, she relives the pain and glory,
And when she dies, it will explain the whole story.

So until then, just keep walking by,
Or give her a smile, she might just reply!

NO COFFEE FOR ME

I won't have caffeine anywhere

OMG I wouldn't dare!

Epilepsy and caffeine don't go together,

Epilepsy and alcohol however!

I'm seizure free since I started drinking whiskey,

But I'll warn you, it makes me frisky!

And Baileys has that special effect,

Within minutes you better become erect.

Drinking a pint of Guinness,

Brings back memories of naughty nights living in Ennis.

Give me a Fat Frog nice and green,

Then I'll bend over the washing machine.

But I'm a lady, so close the door,

Before I get on all four.

See, I don't need medication,

RUNNING FOR MY LIFE

That just puts me under sedation.

All this alcohol keeps me seizure free,

As long as I don't have coffee.

People say epilepsy and alcohol don't mix,

But I'm Irish and I need my daily fix!!!

R U OK

Whilst you cry in pain, I am in too much pain to cry,
Whilst you cry a river, I bleed myself dry.
Whilst your family supports you, mine is nowhere to be seen,
Whilst your support network grows, mine is not even a has been.
Whilst your dog comforts you, mine is 6 foot under,
Whilst your life stands to rise, mine is overpowered by thunder.
Whilst you are surrounded by good friends, I am all alone,
Whilst you call for support, I can't even pick up the phone.
Whilst I am by your side, you are not by mine,
Whilst you show your pain, I pretend to be fine.
Whilst you talk about your issues, I have nobody to tell,
Whilst you live your life, I am dying in this bloodied cell...

RUNNING FOR MY LIFE

Author's Note

To say it has been a challenge to write this memoir is an understatement.

At times, it has been like peeling away the layers of an onion, uncovering deeply buried memories, and delving into old records that have sat for many years locked away.

The process of recalling, examining, and deciding what to include has been cathartic. The fact that I have been able to achieve my dream of finally writing about my past without breaking down and regressing into the dark place I once occupied is a testament to my recovery.

If you are currently travelling a journey where you are facing your own personal challenges, I hope you will find inspiration, courage and understanding that we each have a deep well of resilience within us.

The cover image for this book was deliberately chosen from a photograph I took whilst learning about photography.

I wanted the image to reflect who I am rather than be something generic that held no meaning.

I was walking around Newcastle, and there was nothing on the ground except twigs and leaves, yet amongst them was one red rose. All alone. Nothing else. It was different and struck a chord as it reminded me of myself.

The word LUST is tattooed across the fingers of my right hand and on my left, the word LOVE. Red roses are supposed to represent love.

Holding my camera in my right hand, I positioned the rose carefully in my left so that my rings and fingers with the word love would be visible. The photo, which is basically a selfie of my hand, did not quite work out as I wanted, but it is the perfect choice for my cover.

Love, until Keegan came into my life, has never really existed for me, and yet, despite all I have been through, I still believe in the power of love and the good in humanity.

Designing the cover took me many hours, but as I had nowhere to go during most of the daylight hours, it was a task I took on with gusto.

I am proud to say that it is my own work, once again demonstrating that anything is possible when you are determined to find a way.

If I can do this, anyone can. It is not easy, but it is possible when you are filled with determination and are prepared to look fear in the eye.

Janice Whittle,
Queensland, 2022

Glossary of Terms

ABI: Acquired Brain Injury

AVO: Apprehended Violence Order

BSW: Battered Wife Syndrome

CPTSD: Complex Post Traumatic Stress Disorder

CRS: Commonwealth Rehabilitation Service

EMDR: Eye Movement Desensitisation and Reprocess Therapy

NDIS: National Disability Insurance Scheme

NFR: Not for Resuscitation

TAFE: Technical and Further Education

www.ingramcontent.com/pod-product-compliance
Lightning Source LLC
Chambersburg PA
CBHW050309010526
44107CB00055B/2173